OLD WARDEN
TALES OF
TENANTS & SQUIRES

OLD WARDEN

TALES OF TENANTS & SQUIRES

CHRISTINE A. HILL

AMBERLEY

To my beloved Old Warden
and for its people
past, present and future

If there is a book that you want to read, but it hasn't been written yet, then you must be the one to write it.

Toni Morrison, American writer and novelist

Front Cover Image. 'Old Warden Village',
lithograph by Martin & Hood *c*. 1872 (Bedfordshire & Luton Archives)

First published 2014

Amberley Publishing
The Hill, Stroud
Gloucestershire, GL5 4EP

www.amberley-books.com

British Library Cataloguing in Publication Data.
A catalogue record for this book is available from the British Library.

ISBN 978 1 4456 4058 7 (print)
ISBN 978 1 4456 4091 4 (ebook)

Typesetting and Origination by Amberley Publishing.
Printed in the UK.

Contents

Acknowledgements

I am indebted to:

My mother, Avis Tooke (formerly Fensome, née Marston), who throughout my life has inspired me with so many memories of life in the village we love.

My brother and sister-in-law, Graham and Diana Fensome, for suggesting that I may be interested in doing a bit of research for a village social history project. Seventeen months later, this book is the result.

Michael Marshall of Old Warden parish council for his support and encouragement throughout, and Dawn Marshall for her invaluable help with proofreading.

Villagers past and present: Bob and Jean Bayliss, Cynthia Clarke, Eric Cooper, Robert and Victoria Diggle, Julie Janes, John Jenkins, Bill Foster, Kath Gilbert, June Humphries, Angela Little, Angela Norris, Bob and Dorothy Pearce, Paul Quenby, John and Pat Scott and Cyril Thomas.

Rosemary Sanderson and Rosie Straughair (Swiss Garden), Liz Sutton (Ruby Tiger), Christopher Garrand (Conservation Architect) and Darren Harbar (photographer).

Una Watts and Amanda Done (Shuttleworth Trust) for arranging access to records at Old Warden Park.

Charlotte, Princess Croÿ, Baroness Twickel, Dorothy Shuttleworth's granddaughter.

John and Edmund Wood, Admiral Halsey's grandsons.

Marion Maule, lecturer.

Bob Ricketts for information on Old Warden's postal service.

The kind and patient staff at Bedfordshire and Luton Archives service and The Higgins Art Gallery and Museum.

This publication was made possible due to support from the National Lottery through the Heritage Lottery Fund, and the Shuttleworth Trust, who both sponsored the book.

Thank you all.

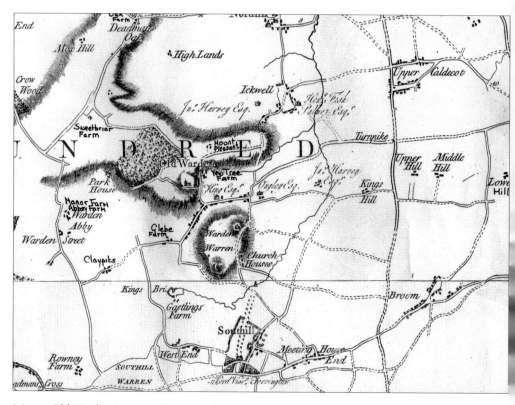

Map 1: Old Warden in 1765 (Thomas Jefferys); some farm names have been superimposed. Ongley's close neighbours were William Smyth King (died 1782) and James Harvey (died 1786), younger brother of John Harvey III of Ickwell Bury.

Map 2: Old Warden Village, from estate sale catalogue, 1872 (Bedfordshire and Luton Archives).

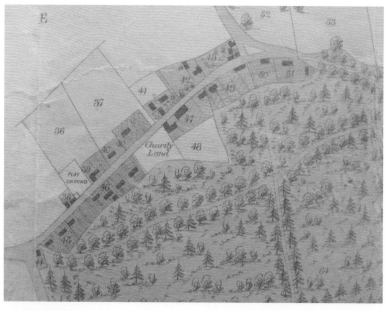

1

The Ongley Squires

Mihi Cura Futuri – I am careful for the future

I have mentioned your inclination to drunkenness and creating a great acquaintance of new companions. All these things are the forerunners of destroying an estate be it never so large and all of them my utter aversion and unless remedied … it will very much lessen my esteem of you and will have a fatal consequence which you will have ye whole time of your life to repention.

Sir Samuel Ongley, threatening to disinherit his nephew, July 1718

I found too on enquiry that this benevolent nobleman does not restrict his attention to external decorations; but that he visits the villagers as their friend, in cases of affliction, and pours oil and wine into their wounds.

Comment on the last Lord Ongley, *Tales, Essays and Poems*, Joseph Gostwick in 1848

Sir Samuel Ongley (1647–1726)

The first Ongley squire was a self-made man of Kent, merchant of London, director of the East India Company, and first deputy governor of the South Seas Co.; he was incredibly rich.

In the mid-1690s, Ongley started to buy up parcels of land and property in the parish of Old Warden and the surrounding villages to create a country estate. He purchased this from the mortgagees of the Bolingbroke family (St John of Bletsoe) and from Sir William Palmer, who owned the red-brick country house and its parkland setting, and he was very rich.

Ongley was a linen draper dealing in fine cloths, and was himself the son of a mercer from Maidstone, where he held another country estate, Vinters. He operated from Mincing Lane and Cornhill, London, where he had homes and warehouses. While in London, he was a common councilman and a freeman of the Merchant Taylors Co., in Maidstone an MP from 1713–15, and in Bedfordshire he was High Sheriff, from 1703–04, and a JP. He was also, as his memorial describes, a governor and benefactor of three hospitals.

In the 1690s, Ongley held a directorship of the East India Company (EIC), which was formed in 1600 to pursue trade with India and Southeast Asia. He also dealt in EIC stock. In 1694, he built and owned a small 210-ton East Indiaman trading ship, the *America*,

The Seat of Lord Ongley, a lithograph by Martin and Hood, *c.* 1872 (Bedfordshire and Luton Archives).

and one voyage is recorded from 1695–97. He was also connected with another ship, the *Anna*, which made three voyages to the East Indies between 1698 and 1709, before it was lost with all hands in the Bay of Bengal.

In 1711, the South Sea Co. was founded as a venture to help reduce the national debt. Ongley became its first Deputy Governor in 1711/12 and he, like many others of the nobility and gentry, invested in the company. Stock rose in value to such a degree that investment frenzy ensued and the infamous South Sea bubble burst in 1720. While thousands were financially ruined by the loss in the stock's value, and others disgraced or impeached for corruption, there is no evidence that Ongley was unduly affected.

In June 1713, Ongley was knighted by Queen Anne, an honour believed to have inspired him to build Queen Anne's summer house. This fine red-brick folly, in Warden Warren, is now restored and managed by the Landmark Trust as a holiday property.

Sir Samuel's commonplace book survives, found in an Upper Caldecote attic. It covers the period from 1712 until his death in 1726, and records copies of leases and land agreements, names of tenants and fields, copies of letters to family, friends and business associates, costings for timber, plastering work, building repairs and property, amounts of rents, notes on forestry management, pruning trees and intriguing recipes and remedies.

Ongley never married, but was a central figure and patriarch in his large extended family. He left his estate to his nephew, Samuel, having earlier taken charge of his education and training for running an estate. This task caused Sir Samuel much anxiety. He grumbled to his nephew at St John's, Oxford, after being asked for more money.

If I had been as you and in the station you are in I should have considered from whom I had
this money. And that this money came as a voluntary gift, not from a parent where there's
some obligation to provide for his own...

In 1720, young Sam left Oxford and had matured enough to work in his uncle's business,
living at the house in Mincing Lane while Sir Samuel lived in retirement at Old Warden.
Sam continued to cause concern, clearly avoiding his uncle's wish for him to marry.

But he has always rejected or evaded the same whenever I pressed him thereunto which makes
me imagine he is either privately married or engaged to marry after my decease with some
inferior fortune.

The Commonplace Book reveals Sir Samuel's stern but ultimately benevolent attitude
towards other relatives who found themselves in financial difficulty, such as Kent cousin,
Sam Fullager, who sought help with a debt of £5,000 owed by his father. Sir Samuel warned,
'kings have long arms and make quick work with those that are indebted to them'.

Whatever the trials and demands placed on him by his family, Sir Samuel maintained the
energy to diligently manage his Bedfordshire and Kent estates. He carefully recorded the
clauses to include his land leases in his book. He was interested in woodland management
and the crops grown on his land. In 1713, he noted that farmer, Nicholas Inskip, was
growing wheat, rye, barley, peas, oats and beans. He was horrified to find 'great neglect
and omission' by parish officials in their failure to maintain regular 'perambulations' of
the parish boundary, the old tradition of beating the bounds where young men could learn
and mark their parish boundaries.

Sir Samuel's memorial stone records that he,

By his indefatigable industry acquired a very plentiful estate, was charitable to the poor, and
very bountiful to his relations. Was free from pride and ostentation, always easy of access and
a kind neighbour, a sincere friend and delighted in doing good offices to all mankind.

Samuel Ongley (1697–1747)

Less than a month after his uncle's death, Sam married Ann Harvey, daughter of John
Harvey of Ickwell Bury. There were no children from the marriage. Sam's sister, Judith,
also married into the Harvey family.

Sam became Tory MP for New Shoreham in Sussex 1729–34, and then Bedford from
1734 until his death in 1747. There is no evidence of his interest in his estates; rather it is
thought that he used his wealth to buy votes in order to further his political career.

There is a note of Sam's good deeds in a newspaper from 1739:

We hear Sir Jeremy Sambroke, Bart, and Samuel Ongley Esquire; the two members for the town of
Bedford, last week had eight oxen killed for the poor of that corporation, 14lb of which was given
to each family, two bushels of coals and a 12*d* loaf: the widows had half this allowance.

Sam died having seemingly left little mark on politics in general and Old Warden in particular. Sir Samuel had looked beyond his nephew's lifetime when making his will, specifying that if Sam died childless then the estates would pass to his nephew-in-law, Robert Henley, and wife, Anne. Anne was the daughter of Sir Samuel's sister, Sarah Merriam. In the event, with the deaths of Robert and Anne Henley and their two eldest sons, the heir became Sir Samuel's great-nephew, Robert Henley. Sir Samuel stipulated that whoever inherited should take the name Ongley, and thus was born the names of the next three Ongley Squires; all of them were named Robert Henley Ongley.

Robert Henley Ongley, 1st Baron Ongley (1721–85)

The third member of the Ongley dynasty brought a barony to Old Warden and provided a direct line of heirs. Little is known of his early life, apart from him being a barrister at law in London. In 1763, he married Frances Gosfright, co-heiress to London merchant Richard Gosfright, of Langton Hall, Essex. Upon marrying, Frances may well have brought with her a similar fortune to that of her sister Sarah, which was said to be £25,000. They had two sons and four daughters: Frances (1764–1823), unmarried and buried in Eversholt; Catherine, born in 1766 and married John Edwards Fremantle in 1790; Ann (1767–1810), unmarried and buried in Old Warden; Sarah, born in 1770 and married William Phillimore in 1791; Robert, born in 1771 and married Frances Burgoyne of Sutton Park, Bedfordshire; Samuel, born in 1774 and married Frances Monoux of Sandye Place, Bedfordshire.

A career in politics beckoned and, supported by the Duke of Bedford, Ongley became a Whig MP for Bedford in 1754. There followed a long spell as MP for Bedfordshire from 1761 until 1780. He was also an active JP, regularly dispensing justice at the county quarter sessions, and a Guardian of the Thomas Coram Foundling Hospital, London, between the 1750s and the 1770s.

There are mixed reports of Ongley's skills and allegiances as a politician. His parliamentary speeches did not appear to influence or convince. A description of him in 1779 says: 'He is a very narrow-minded, selfish man and a tedious bad speaker.' Other reports of his parliamentary career indicate arrogance about his wealth and little empathy for the poor. He was accused of being parsimonious and 'purse-proud'. This trait may be reflected in an epic political satire of the time, *The Rolliad*, when Samuel Whitbread and Ongley were neatly compared:

> Whitbread and Ongley,
> pride of Bedford's vale
> This fam'd for selling,
> that for saving ale

In 1776, his services to parliament were rewarded with an Irish barony, which enabled him to continue sitting as an MP in the Commons. His full title was Baron Ongley of Old

The Ongley Mausoleum, Thomas Fisher 1772–1836 (Bedfordshire and Luton Archives).

Warden in Ireland. Ongley did not stand for re-election in 1780, due to a clash with Lord Ossory. Both Ossory and Ongley were nominated to stand as members for Bedfordshire, but Ossory declined to be a joint candidate with Ongley, who duly made an announcement in the press regarding this decision, saying: 'I perceived an unnatural conjunction of parties against me; which it was impossible to item, without the most powerful assistance.' On the same day Ossory announced that he was standing with St Andrew St John (14th Baron St John of Bletsoe).

In 1784, the year before Ongley died, came a disputed election and an end to Ongley's long political career. He stood again for parliament after a four-year break, and the poll results showed that St Andrew St John had a one vote majority. Ongley challenged the vote, and the matter ended up as an enquiry in Westminster Hall. St John eventually won after a counter petition in 1785, and accusations of bribery were levelled against Ongley. The case had backfired against him, for, whether bribery was involved or not, in 1784, the committee had found that the vote of William Lugsden for Ongley had been incorrectly added to St John's votes. This was corrected and the seat was given to Ongley. However, when St John counter-petitioned, a vote for both St John and Ossory was found to have been given only to Ossory. When this was likewise corrected the outcome of the vote remained in St John's favour.

Little is known of Ongley's contribution to his Old Warden estate, but the one visible legacy is the Ongley Mausoleum, built in 1790 by Frances, Dowager Lady Ongley, carrying out instructions in her husband's will.

Robert Henley Ongley, 2nd Baron Ongley (1771–1814)

The 2nd Baron inherited the title at the tender age of fourteen. He was educated at Westminster School and Trinity College, Cambridge, where he gained an MA in 1790.

John Byng, the diarist, made pithy comments about the young Ongley in 1790: 'By Ld O's dog kennel: ignorance of youth.' In 1794, Byng saw Ongley and 'Mr P' out exercising their hunters. He commented 'What folly! Gallop after your hounds and your horses will be exercised. But these new systems are founded in fashion, and having no other basis quickly fade away.'

In 1801, Ongley married Frances Burgoyne, daughter of professional soldier Maj.-Gen. Sir John Burgoyne of Sutton Park, Bedfordshire. There were seven children from this marriage, and their brief stories are at the end of this chapter: Robert (born 1803), Samuel Trench (born 1806), Montagu (born 1808), George (born 1809), Frederick (born 1810), Frances (born 1813) and Charlotte (born 1814).

The 2nd Baron did not inherit his father's interests in politics, and was very different in character. Contemporary newspapers painted a picture of a man committed to farming his country estate (described as an 'agricultural gentleman') and socialising with his county peers, such as the Duke of Bedford and Samuel Whitbread.

His farming interests included the raising of Southdown sheep, Scotch Oxen (Highland cattle) and pigs. Every autumn, Joshua Maldon, the local Biggleswade auctioneer, arranged a sale of Ongley's livestock, which always took place at Lord Ongley's Farm near the church – Yew Tree Farm (Nos 1/2 Church End).

This was the period of big names in agriculture, such as Thomas Coke of Holkham and Francis, 5th Duke of Bedford, men who led the way in developing agricultural productivity. Landowners were continuing the process of enclosure, doing away with the old strips of open and common field systems in order, they said, to support more efficient farming methods.

Ongley showed interest in agricultural competition, inventions and improvements, attending the nationally important annual Woburn Sheep Shearing Fair, occasionally winning prizes and watching demonstrations of new agricultural equipment. He introduced the two-horse (or four-oxen) threshing machine to Old Warden. Needing less manpower than traditional flailing, there was no doubt that there was a mixture of fascination and concern among his labourers – new technology meaning fewer jobs.

Ongley was diligent in his responsibilities to his country. In 1794, he subscribed £200 towards raising a regiment of infantry in London and, in 1798, together with Mr Trevor (of Bromham) and Samuel Whitbread, he raised a troop of yeomanry in the county. He was also a deputy lieutenant of Bedfordshire. He did his duty in the care of the poor, such as spending £14 on bread and beef for the poor of Warden in the cold January of 1795. The following week, he bought a fat beast from St Ives market to be distributed with bread and coals.

He followed the trend of rationalising his estates by exchanging parcels of land with neighbour Samuel Whitbread, in order to create a more compact landholding. It is thought that he was responsible for laying out the park around Old Warden House around 1800–05. In 1802, a Road Order shows that he diverted the road running through the park, close to the house through what was to become the Swiss Garden (see map 1). A new section of road was made between the turn for Ickwell at Colemoreham, running down 'aerodrome hill' to meet up with the road to Biggleswade. It is possible that Ongley started planning a garden at the boggy site of the Swiss Garden after changing the layout of the road, but there is no firm evidence for this.

He died in 1814, his heir a child of just eleven and baby Charlotte born two months before his death. His younger brother, Samuel Ongley of Sandye Place, gave the reason for Ongley's comparatively early death, contributing to a publication in 1823 on the best remedies for gout: 'the Hon. S. Ongley has suffered from frequent and severe fits of gout during many years. Gout is hereditary in his family, his brother, the late Lord Ongley, having died of it at the age of forty-three.'

Robert Henley Ongley, 3rd Baron Ongley (1803–77)

Inheriting at such a young age, in the guardianship of his mother and with six younger siblings, this boy would grow up to leave a lasting legacy in Old Warden.

He was educated by a larger than life character, Revd Dr Thomas Redman Hooker, at his school in Rottingdean, Sussex, alongside another of the Ongley boys – likely the next in age – Samuel Trench. Hooker was a 'hunting parson' who took 'a few young men of fashion under his roof, whom, if they will not be made scholars, he is certain to make gentlemen', and the school was reputed to have more sons of the nobility than any other. Hooker was an educated and clever man, but also thought to act as look-out for the Rottingdean gang of smugglers, his expert speed on a horse enabling him to give a quick warning should the revenue men be about. Ongley must have had an interesting time here.

The choice of school may have reflected Ongley's lack of academic ability, for his brothers, Frederick and George, went to Eton. However, Rottingdean was conveniently close to Brighton, where the dowager Lady Ongley was often included in the social melee at the court of the Prince Regent, later George IV.

View past the thatched tree seat towards the Swiss Cottage, *c.* 1900 (The Shuttleworth Trust).

In 1822, Ongley matriculated from Christ Church College, Oxford, with the help of private tutor William Otter, later the Bishop of Chichester. Whether he was sent on a grand tour after this, or simply returned to Old Warden to manage his estates, is not known, but at some stage in the 1820s he began his plans for a landscaped Swiss garden, a model village and later a complete a refurbishment of St Leonard's church.

Hints at the motivation, if not the influences, behind Ongley's work on his estate, appear in an 1854 Select Committee report for the House of Lords, the researcher having visited the village and talked directly with the people:

> Chairman: Was it Lord Ongley who looked after the people? The answer was 'yes'; the people all wore red handkerchiefs like the Swiss, and it was his lordship's hobby to have the village look like a Swiss village.

There is no evidence that Ongley visited Switzerland, but his mother certainly travelled extensively, as reported in newspapers, for example taking two of her sons to Italy in 1835 to visit the Sistine Chapel for example. Mavis Batey says in her article 'An English View of Switzerland' (Country Life, 17 February 1977) that the 1820s saw interest in the Alps develop after Europe opened up at the conclusion of the Napoleonic Wars. As a family of fashion, the Ongley's would have followed suit – and she considered that Ongley was probably influenced by J. B. Papworth's book *Hints on Ornamental Gardening*, published in 1823.

The young Ongley was of course very familiar with the taste and style of the Prince Regent, the family being regular visitors to Brighton and the Royal Pavilion, mingling with the Prince's social set.

There are also hints that in his new garden he wanted to create a memorial, perhaps to his father, his brother Samuel-Trench (who died in 1826), or – as in village folklore – to a lost love, his 'Swiss mistress'. The themes of Romanticism, the Picturesque and melancholy pervade the garden, the last underlined by poems of loss on two inscribed tablets.

On a practical level, much groundwork needed to be done to create the ponds and little hills, the buildings and the planting, and he used local labourers, as a newspaper recorded in 1832:

> The Swiss Cottage, about half a mile from the house, a beautiful building situated in the midst of a perfectly fairy ground, which his Lordship has formed from time to time according to his own taste, to the great advantage of his poor tenantry, who have thus been kept in continual employment.

Towards the end of the 1820s, Ongley was also remodelling Old Warden village described variously as in the Picturesque, Rustic or Cottage Orné style popular in the eighteenth century and early nineteenth century. Using woodland and shrubbery as a picturesque backdrop Old Warden, already a pretty village in its gentle valley sheltered by the wooded warren, was an ideal subject for this treatment. A local newspaper from February 1830 reported:

> We have sincere pleasure in being able to record the munificent acts of a young nobleman, Lord Ongley … The cottages in the village have all been repaired at his Lordship's expense, both internally and externally; clothing of every description has been liberally distributed

under his Lordship's direction ... Improvements are still in progress, and great part of his Lordship's time, most of which is spent at his country mansion, is occupied in the laudable process of ameliorating the conditions of the poor.

Ongley was as obsessive about detailing in the village as he was in his Swiss Garden. The clothing he gave to the villagers is surely a direct reference to the red cloaks and tall hats he wanted them to wear, so that they themselves would become part of the picturesque scene which would greet him, and his visitors, when passing through.

Gillian Darley in her book, *Villages of Vision* (1978), wrote:

The truly Picturesque feature of Old Warden is the care with which the cottages are placed, surrounded by hedges and trees which are the result of a very fully planned exercise in planting ... The cottages suggest a village where the hand of some leading Picturesque architect might be traced, perhaps P. F. Robinson who had worked with Holland at Southill nearby.

Peter Frederick Robinson wrote in *Village Architecture* (1830): 'There is no way in which wealth can produce such natural unaffected variety, as by adorning a real village, and promoting the comforts and enjoyments of its inhabitants.' He could have been writing about Ongley.

Ongley's beautification of St Leonard's church came in 1841/42. It was fitted with High Church carvings from the Low Countries and Italy, again reflecting Ongley's own taste. The churchyard was landscaped similarly to the Swiss Garden and the village, clearly seen

The Thatched House, a typical Ongley rustic cottage in the centre of the village, *c*. 1890. Deceptively, it was formerly three dwellings.

Victorian print of St Leonard's church,
Old Warden.

in the remaining yews and cypresses. Inscribed tablets were placed at the entrance gate and on the path to the chancel, with a biblical quote above the old church porch.

By 1851, Ongley had tenants in Old Warden House, the first being George E. Russell, a former EIC civil servant, followed by Charles Tanqueray and finally, in 1871, by Henry Browning. Ongley left the village for good around 1854. The money was running out.

There had been problems with his father's final will, which resulted in an earlier will (from 1801) being used that made no provision for his large family – a responsibility falling to the new lord when he came of age. As well as the expense of his building, landscaping and ornamentation projects, he was buying up land to add to the estate. In 1844, he spent £8,000 on 183 acres, including Wood Farm and Park Farm. Over the period 1837–50, he took out mortgages of £45,000. In 1861, he paid off the debts owed, but then took out a fresh mortgage of £16,000.

Press reports add further understanding of the spending and of the family lifestyle. In 1820/21, young Ongley commissioned an expensive dessert service from the Derby porcelain factory, considered 'one of the most costly ever got up'. Known today as 'the Ongley Service', it is housed at Muncaster Castle in Cumbria.

In 1829, during his village and garden works, a series of letters between Sir John Osborn of Chicksands and Revd Edmond Williamson of Campton refer to Lady Ongley's efforts to get a donation from her son towards a good cause. She confided to Lady Osborn that her son was 'extremely pinched for money and has sold off some property to clear off some incumbrances so that he cannot at the present moment supply, although he has every disposition to help us'.

The Ongley family were all devotees of hunting, horse racing and horse breeding – as expensive a sport then as it is now. The brothers could be found at Leamington Spa for the season, out with the Warwickshire Hunt and at the racetrack. They also frequented the Oakley Hunt, Huntingdon races, Newmarket , Epsom and Bedford Races at Cow Meadow, the latter running the 'Warden Stakes' with the prize being 5 sovereigns and a silver cup.

Ongley bred game fowl to participate in a passion of the age – cockfighting. He was said to be one of the greatest patrons of the Royal Cockpit in Tufton Street, London, a place where the great and good mixed equally with the lowest of London's life. These sports must have taken their toll on Ongley's finances, but were probably seen as a necessary part of being a nobleman of fashion.

Coventry was a famed horse, both for his high step trotting action when pulling a buggy, and for the huge sum of money Ongley paid for him, likely in the tens of thousands in today's money. The *New Sporting Magazine* made reference to Coventry in 1831:

No-one will suppose that the celebrated buggy horse, Coventry, for which if I mistake not, Lord Ongley gave about 1,000 guineas, was intrinsically worth that sum; for, whatever might be his symmetry, his action could not bear anything like a relative proportion to the price, and if a buggy horse can be purchased for £40 which can trot 12 or 14 miles an hour in harness, what more could Coventry do, even if the owner had given 10,000 guineas for him?

Coventry, the property of the Rt. Hon Lord Ongley, 1824, from an engraving by William Fellowes.

A court case against Ongley in 1860 (*see Chapter 4*) made mockery of Ongley's spending. His former horse dealer said: 'His Lordship had a large stud of the finest horses in London. He gave 700 guineas for a cab horse, and afterwards I bought him a better horse for 90 guineas.' At the hearing, Ongley admitted that he was not much of a businessman and that a former groom was always troubling him for money but he just paid him.

Ongley had a kind and generous nature and his tenants were well cared for, even if they had to wear clothes of his choosing and maintain the appearance of their picturesque cottages and gardens. An example of his approachability and care towards seventy-seven-year-old Samuel Goodship, the village rabbit catcher, is in a newspaper report from 1843:

> A cottager of the name of Goodship was found dead in his bed. He had no person to live with him, but a neighbour was in the habit of attending to his domestic matters. He complained on Saturday morning of a sensation of choking, and his neighbour went to Lord Ongley's house to ask for a little honey for him. She administered a portion of honey and vinegar to the poor man, but not finding him relieved she went again and told Lord Ongley, who accompanied her to the cottage. His Lordship went upstairs and found that the poor man had just breathed his last.

This poem was found in the church visitor books signed by Ongley's friend and hunting companion Lt-Col. Robert H. Lowth, 86th Regiment. Dated 21 July 1854, it seems to signify Ongley's final departure from Old Warden.

> A distant part of thy native land
> Writes this memorial with grateful hand
> Blest be the heart which takes such pains to prove
> The faithful tribute of his Christian love
> Long live Lord Ongley, Wardens rising star
> Seen by the pilgrims travelling from afar
> Here would he rest – but if it may not be
> God grant to Ongley, he His Rest may see
> Farewell good Lord, thy work on earth stands fast
> Pardon this tribute from a servant's hand
> My master is the Lord of every land
> He sees me write and knows the word I speak
> And his commands I would not ever break
> But writing this delighted on I move
> Remembering only Ongleys sacred love.

In the same year there was a large auction of Ongley's farming stock, agricultural implements, and other items.

Ongley eventually leased a fourteen-bedroom house, Bushey Lodge in Teddington, standing directly opposite the entrance to Bushey Park. His interest in gardens continued, for when Bushey Lodge was put up for lease after his death, the advert said, 'the pleasure grounds have been laid out with exquisite taste and at a very great cost, and the kitchen garden is very productive with forcing houses, melon pits etc.'

In 1871, George Ongley (heir to the Barony) died, which was probably the catalyst for the estate being sold in 1872. Ongley himself died on 21 January 1877, and is buried in the family mausoleum. Like his father, he'd suffered from chronic gout for fifteen years, his death certificate also citing 'atrophy of the brain' for two months before he died. With his eye for detail and care for people, Ongley's will listed forty-seven bequests and legacies. He included people from Old Warden (see later chapters) and remembered all of his servants, however humble. He had been worth around £180,000, but £165,000 had come from the sale of Old Warden.

What happened to the Henley Ongley heirs? Samuel-Trench was an ensign and lieutenant in the Grenadier Guards. He died in Ireland in 1826, aged only twenty-three and has a memorial in Dublin's Holy Trinity Cathedral. The unusual Trench element of his name originated from his maternal grandmother's second husband.

Montagu was a captain in the Coldstream Guards. In 1856, he died unmarried in Harrogate aged forty-seven. He suffered from chronic bronchitis and cerebral congestion, and was probably taking the waters at the Harlow sulphurous alkaline springs and baths when he died. Thomas Morgan of Old Warden, family servant and George Ongley's stud groom, was present at his death.

George was also a captain in the Coldstream Guards. He never married and settled at Mount Pleasant House, Old Warden, where he lived alone with several servants. After his army service he became a farmer and horse breeder, taking in Cold Harbour (then called Wood Farm) and Oak Farm at Moxhill. He was the last heir to the Ongley Barony, predeceasing Lord Ongley in 1871.

Frederick was a lieutenant in the Royal Horseguards and was just thirty-five and a bachelor when he died in 1846 at Old Warden. He'd suffered a second attack of apoplexy, probably a heart attack or stroke.

Frances outlived all her siblings and was with Lord Ongley when he died at Bushey Lodge. Her husband, Barff Tucker, was a talented artist who was killed tragically in the Italian War of Independence in 1859. They had no children and Frances never remarried, living independently at a small farm in Waltham St Lawrence, Berkshire, where she took in lady boarders.

Charlotte was the only Ongley to have children. In 1837, she married Capt. Charles W. P. Magra of the 21st Fusiliers. He was later declared bankrupt, spending time in debtor's prison. The marriage failed, he deserted Charlotte and divorce followed. There were two sons, Charles Francis Henley Ongley Magra and Henley Oxford Magra, no doubt named in the hope of eventual inheritance. In 1879, Henley died aged thirty-nine and unmarried. In 1864, Charles was imprisoned for bankruptcy but picked himself up and became a vaccination officer for Hounslow Poor Law Union, rising to sanitary inspector and inspector of nuisances (dumped rubbish, cesspits) for Hounslow Borough. He married and had three children. A daughter died in infancy, son Henley George Magra died aged six and Charles Magra died aged seventeen, the last of the Henley Ongley line.

2

The Shuttleworth Squires

Isto Velocoir Vita – Thither is life swifter

Shuttleworth ... is one of the iron kings or merchant princes of Lincoln, having literally risen from a common labourer.

Col Weston Cracroft (1815–83)

Suddenly, at last, it seemed to come into my mind to make an agricultural college to train young men and help to get them jobs and show them a good way of life.

Dorothy Shuttleworth, 1942

Joseph Shuttleworth (1819–83)

Joseph Shuttleworth, iron founder and industrialist of Lincoln, purchased the Old Warden estate at the age of fifty-three and became its squire and benefactor for eleven productive years. Like Sir Samuel Ongley before him, he was a self-made man of great wealth, and he came with the intention of spending it.

Joseph's father, John Allenby Shuttleworth, was a boat builder at Dogdyke, on the banks of the Witham near Coningsby. His son followed the family trade by becoming a shipwright and living at Waterside, Lincoln. In 1842, Joseph married Sarah Grace Clayton, sister of Nathaniel Clayton, who operated horse-drawn packet ships and had an iron foundry at Stamp End on the Witham, next to Shuttleworth's boatyard. The two men, united by marriage, location and mutual business interests, formed the partnership of Clayton & Shuttleworth.

Operating from their Stamp End works, the firm prospered, largely due to the production of portable and fixed steam engines for use in agricultural tasks such as threshing and winnowing. The 1851 Great Exhibition successfully promoted their business and, by the 1860s, they were making steam cultivating machinery, combined threshing and winnowing machines, straw elevators, corn grinding mills, flour dressing machines, circular saw benches, irrigation pumps and many other items. Investing in new products, the firm was soon able to open branches in a number of European cities, including Vienna, where Joseph's brother, John Shuttleworth, took charge.

Joseph's success opened the door into Lincoln society. He was a member of the city council and elected mayor in 1858/59. He was a magistrate, JP and a deputy-lieutenant of

Left: Caroline Shuttleworth, from a portrait by Henry Richard Graves RA (The Shuttleworth Trust).

Right: Joseph Shuttleworth from a portrait by Frank Holl RA, 1882 (The Shuttleworth Trust).

the city, member of the Council of the Royal Agricultural Society and on the Board of the Great Northern Railway.

In 1849, Sarah Grace died, leaving him with two young sons, Alfred and Frank. In 1861, he married Caroline Jane Ellison (born 1836), daughter of Col Richard Ellison of Boultham Hall, Lincoln. There is indication that people thought the couple were mismatched. Caroline was seventeen years younger than her husband, and Joseph's humble background may have seemed unsuitable. However, the marriage was said to be happy and Caroline was to prove a worthy wife and stepmother.

By 1861, the business was employing 900 men, and Shuttleworth's growing wealth and status enabled him to look for a grander house. He failed to secure the purchase of Lord Byron's Newstead Abbey, so instead he bought the lake and grounds of the Lincoln Waterworks Co. at Hartsholme on the outskirts of Lincoln. The architect Maj. F. H. Goddard was commissioned to build his new house, Hartsholme Hall, and the acclaimed landscape designer Edward Milner (1819–84) landscaped the grounds, with work starting in 1862. Milner had worked at Chatsworth under Joseph Paxton, and would later come to Old Warden to landscape the park and supervise the restoration of the Swiss Garden and wider estate. Hartsholme was demolished in the 1950s, the grounds becoming a successful country park.

In early 1872, Joseph purchased the Old Warden estate from Lord Ongley and proceeded to set himself up as a landed gentleman; his new country estate enabled his family to engage in game shooting and house parties, which had been popularised by the Prince of Wales.

He started work immediately after his purchase was complete. Warden House, thought to have been built around 1610, had a tenant whose lease expired in 1875; Joseph had to wait before he could pull the old house down and redevelop the site. Just one Ongley building was retained here, an eighteenth-century timber and red-brick barn, now restored and used as offices. The established architect Henry Clutton was commissioned to design the new house and stable block, two new Jacobean-style lodges with park gates, and the new village school. Elsewhere in Bedfordshire, Clutton had designed St Mary's church, Woburn and Sandy Lodge, current headquarters of the RSPB.

The imposing new house is strikingly similar to the Elizabethan Gawthorpe Hall, Lancashire, by no coincidence the ancestral home of an eminent branch of Shuttleworths, with a line going back at least to the fourteenth century. Joseph also adopted the image of a gloved hand holding a shuttle as his family crest, the same device appearing in the coat of arms of the Tudor Shuttleworths of Gawthorpe. There is no proven link between Gawthorpe and the Lincolnshire Shuttleworths, but Joseph possibly wanted to portray that common desire of 'new money' – a history and ancestry for his own family.

After 180 years of Ongley ownership, the village was full of expectation and rumour about the new owner. At the parish vestry meeting, in April 1872, comment was made on the 'unsettled state of the parish' resulting from the sale of the estate. Decisions on a new school were deferred to await the leadership (and largesse) of the new squire, and Joseph's name was expediently added to the committee of management.

The village was not disappointed, with the scope and vigour of work that Joseph undertook to redress the neglect during the final Ongley years. He upgraded the farms, building a new wing at Mount Pleasant and ordered Edward Milner to plan new gardens, both here and at Hill Farm. He auctioned all the old farm buildings and equipment at Mount Pleasant and Hill Farm (1872), Home Farm (1875), and Yew Tree Farm (1877). At Yew Tree, a lovely new granary was built and the old farmhouse was given a typical Shuttleworth makeover.

Designs were commissioned for the refurbishment of the labourers' cottages in and around the village, and for some new cottages. He added his own particular style in the form of decorative half timbering to the exterior of some original Ongley cottages. On a practical level he improved sanitation by adding substantial wash houses and outside 'privies', and gave the village a new communal bakehouse. He built a new gamekeeper's cottage and kennels next to Queen Anne's summer house (both Landmark Trust holiday properties). In the new design for his park entrance two Ongley buildings were lost, the original rustic lodge at the old park gates, set further back into the park, and also 'Brick Nog' Cottage, timber-framed with brick infill.

Clayton & Shuttleworth designed a new blacksmith's shop at the rear of No. 32 the Village, to replace the old smithy buildings at Parsonage Piece, and their decorative iron railings fronted the Hare & Hounds and its stables (now the Clock House). The firm also provided items, such as the bell chamber and clock case, for the clock tower of Joseph's new house.

A new laundry to serve Joseph's household was established at Vicarage (Glebe) Farm in Bedford Road, now Laundry Farm. It had a washroom with washing tubs, a large ironing room, mangles, starch tub and a hot closet, with a fireplace next to a coal store and, of course, drying racks and posts.

The gardens received significant and sympathetic attention. Research carried out in advance of the twentieth-century restorations of Swiss Garden shows that Shuttleworth embarked on major repairs to the Swiss Cottage, grotto and fernery, the thatched tree seat, punt harbour and underpass as well as adding the pond cascade bridge, which was made by Clayton & Shuttleworth. Extensive use was made of the artificial rock, Pulhamite,

Gawthorpe Hall.

Old Warden Park.

much loved by the Victorians. Joseph's interest in gardens was reflected in his presidency of the Sandy Floral & Horticultural Society.

In January 1883, he died at Hartsholme after a long illness during which two eminent physicians, Sir William Gull and Sir William Jenner, were consulted. Despite Lincolnshire being the place of his birth, and rise to wealth and status, he chose to be buried at Old Warden in a new family vault. Alfred Shuttleworth inherited the Lincolnshire estates, and Frank the Old Warden and Goldington estates.

Caroline Shuttleworth, still relatively young at forty-seven, stayed in Old Warden fulfilling the duties of chatelaine for Frank. She developed a strong bond with the village, regularly visiting the school, spoiling the children, and issuing books to commemorate Queen Victoria's Jubilee. At the first school treat after her death, the Revd Lang referred to the deep personal interest that Caroline had always taken in the children and how everybody missed her – she had clearly been a regular figure at these treats and was much loved.

In 1899, she died of pneumonia at Old Warden. A large memorial statue was erected by her sister in the church, above the Shuttleworth family pew, and Frank donated a window to her memory.

Frank Shuttleworth (1845–1913)

Frank attended Dr Lovell's liberal multilingual school at Winslow Hall, Buckinghamshire, completing his education in France and Germany. He then embarked on a career in the Army, joining the cavalry units of the 11th, and then 7th, Hussars. Advanced to major in 1882, the death of his father caused him to retire after serving for eighteen years, the first four of those in India. There are no tales of daring exploits on active service although, in India, he seemed to have enjoyed big game hunting.

For the next twenty years, Frank lived the life of a wealthy bachelor squire based at Old Warden. As a Bedfordshire landowner he became a JP, and was High Sheriff in 1891. His business interests included his directorship of Clayton & Shuttleworth and the Great Northern Railway. Locally, Frank was chairman of the Old Warden parish council, president of the cricket club, a churchwarden and county council member for Northill, Southill and Old Warden.

Frank continued the work of his father in caring for the estate and its buildings. In 1887, he gave the church a new organ to celebrate the Diamond Jubilee of Queen Victoria, housing it in an enlarged vestry. In 1899, the church bells were recast. He brought a new pulpit from an antique shop in Edinburgh to replace Lord Ongley's old 'double-decker', and endowed the church with several memorial windows.

Horses were as major a part of his life as they had been in his Army days. He ran a horse stud, breeding shire horses, hunters and thoroughbreds, showing them across the country, entering them in steeplechases, and often riding them himself and winning prizes. He was a member of the Four in Hand Club and Master of the Cambridgeshire Fox Hounds. Owning a succession of yachts Frank was elected a member of the elite Royal Yacht Squadron, based at Cowes, in 1888. In the Cowes Week of 1894, Frank was present at the visit of 'Kaiser Bill', witnessing all the pomp and ceremony surrounding the Kaiser and his relatives, the British

Frank Shuttleworth, from a portrait by Walter William Ouless RA, 1904 (The Shuttleworth Trust)

Royal Family. His yacht guestbook has many interesting entries: the commanding officers from the Kaiser's yacht, the Meteor, the Empress Eugenie of France, Prince Arthur, the Infante Alfonso of Spain and local friends which included the Diggle and Whitbread families.

In 1901, he accepted the role of commanding officer of the newly formed Beds Imperial Yeomanry; all its soldiers were required to be able horsemen. He took the honorary title of colonel, and from then on was known as Colonel Shuttleworth.

In complete contrast to the society circles in which he moved, Frank took pleasure in his responsibilities to the people in his village and his duties as squire. He held annual school treats in the park for the village children, when he would give each child a present. He happily took part in village entertainments; in 1897, the parish magazine reporting that Frank 'recited "On the Beach" and sang Lord H. Somerset's song "Across the Blue Sea"'. At the same event, the vicar's young daughter also contributed, 'Miss D. C. Lang played "Griegs Wachterlied" and her brothers performed on the piano.' She would soon play a significant role in Frank's life.

To the villagers' delight, Frank's engagement to Miss Dorothy Clotilda Lang, daughter of the vicar of Old Warden, was announced in April 1902. Frank was fifty-seven and Dorothy twenty-three, a cause for parental concern and subject of village gossip.

Dorothy was raised in an ecclesiastical family. Her father, Revd Robert Lang, and mother, Adine Louisa Tayler, were both born in India. 'Bob' Lang was a first-class cricketer for Cambridge University from 1860–62, gaining fame as a fast bowler. He was ordained in 1863, and after a series of livings became vicar of Silsoe (1873–87). He then took a role in the Church Missionary Society (CMS) as group secretary for Palestine and Africa, involving some travel abroad. In 1892, he became the vicar of Old Warden.

Born in Silsoe in 1879, Dorothy was a young girl of thirteen by the time her family took up residence in the Vicarage House at Old Warden (now Orchard Grange). The youngest daughter of a family of seven, she had four older brothers and a sister, and one younger brother. Of her brothers, two became vicars, one an Army colonel and another a headmaster.

Her early years in the village included the genteel activities of her mother, which were geared to her father's religious interests and position. The parish magazines make clear the family's continued commitment to the CMS, fundraising and promoting the cause of missionaries abroad. Dorothy would have known Frank well, as her father was a significant figure in parish affairs and Frank was involved with village welfare. Quite how her relationship with Frank developed is not known, but Joyce Last, niece of the Shuttleworth cook Fanny Cave, often stayed as a guest at Old Warden Park in the 1930s, and remembered Dorothy saying that she and the colonel used to do their courting in the Swiss Garden – appropriate in such a romantic setting. She was known as 'the sunbeam of Old Warden and light of the village', according to her brother, Arthur Lang.

The couple married in June 1902, Dorothy's father performing the ceremony and the Beds Imperial Yeomanry forming a guard of honour. The churchyard was filled with hundreds of people 'of all classes'.

After their honeymoon in Paris, the couple's homecoming was marked by further festivities, with a yeomanry escort from Biggleswade station and a rendition of 'Home Sweet Home'. The welcome by the villagers is described in local newspapers:

Arches of flags and evergreen spanned the one main thoroughfare and houses were gaily bedecked with flowers and bunting of bright and party-colours. At the entrance to the Hall ... Long lines of decorations were placed on each side of the gateway, and over it was placed a triumphal arch, surmounted by crowns, and in the centre was the significant word 'Welcome' ... At the entrance to the Vicarage, the old home of Mrs Shuttleworth, was erected an arch, on the left hand side, on which was printed in white letters on a scarlet ground the words 'Welcome Adieu'. The only inn of the village – the Hare & Hounds – looked more inviting than usual with its profuse display of bunting.

After her marriage, Dorothy's parents moved away from Old Warden, and Robert Lang became vicar of Dinton, Bucks, and then vicar of Woodham Walter, Essex, in 1907 where he died in 1908.

Frank's pride in his new wife was clear. In 1904, a portrait of Dorothy by Frank Dicksee RA was exhibited at the Royal Academy, one of many beautiful portraits commissioned by her husband.

By 1905, Frank was winding down his activities. He had already ceased his role as Master of Foxhounds and he now stepped down from the yeomanry. The press reported that

Colonel & Mrs Shuttleworth are both devoted to country life and spend most of their time at Old Warden Park ... They do not go in for much entertaining now, though at one time Col Shuttleworth was a prominent figure in society and used to drive a four-in-hand.

A two-month spring cruise of the Mediterranean, in 1905, was followed the next year by a four-month world tour. Dorothy maintained a diary and the Japanese leg of the tour has now been published – *A Visit to Japan in 1906*.

The long-awaited heir arrived in 1909, and was christened Richard Ormonde. The choice of the baby's first name may have been a further nod to the Gawthorpe Shuttleworth's, Richard being the name of the firstborn son of that line from the early 1500s to the 1700s. The name Ormonde came from his godfather, Lord Ormonde. Richard did not get to know his father well for Frank's heart was failing, and he died in January 1913.

Dorothy Shuttleworth as Trustee (1913–32)

At the very outset of war on 6 August 1914, Dorothy remarried. Her new husband was Brig.-Gen. William MacClaren Campbell (1864–1924), a family friend who had previously been a guest at house and shooting parties. He was an army man, joining the Black Watch in 1883, seeing active service in Burma and South Africa and, in 1899, serving as aide-de-camp to George Curzon, Viceroy of India. There is suggestion that he hated his career, but an obituary describes him as a 'vigorous and attractive personality, of great charm of manner and person and of decided military abilities'. Just a few days after their marriage, Campbell resumed command of the 2nd Battalion of Black Watch bound for France, where he served in the trenches in 1914/15.

Dorothy, with typical vigour, addressed herself to the war effort. In August 1914, along with other Bedfordshire property owners, she volunteered Old Warden Park to the Beds branch of the British Red Cross Society, and it became a convalescent hospital for wounded soldiers. She also offered her London townhouse, although there is no record that this was taken up. In 1915, Dorothy took in Belgian refugees, fleeing from the German occupation of their country.

In August 1917, Dorothy's only daughter was born – Anne Elspeth Campbell – who married an Austrian, Alexander, Prince von Croÿ, in 1938. Throughout 1918, Dorothy served as a voluntary part-time unpaid nurse at Kempston Auxiliary Hospital, which housed seventy beds for wounded soldiers.

Her husband survived his time at the Front, but, after 1915, had returned to England when his health broke down as a result of his experiences in trench warfare. He was a victim of shell shock, a phenomenon new to medical science and widely misunderstood. For men affected, particularly those of high rank such as Campbell, the impact could be devastating, as people were suspicious that cowardice and weakness were behind

A miniature portrait of Dorothy Shuttleworth, *c.* 1903. The tiara was a present from her husband (Emma, Countess von Waldburg-Wolfegg).

an affected individual's behaviour. Wives may have suffered shame, embarrassment, confusion and anger at what had happened to their husbands.

Campbell never made a full recovery and, in 1924, died suddenly in Brussels. It was said that the marriage had not been happy, but with the conditions of war keeping them apart and Campbell's poor health, the chance of happiness may have simply eluded them. Dorothy later changed her name back to Shuttleworth by deed poll, feeling it more practical for running the estate.

Dorothy was also busy introducing her young son to the duties of squire. Still a child, Master Richard was regularly taken to the village school to meet the children and carry out little duties such as giving out presents at Christmas and even providing entertainment.

Once life had settled down after the war, improvements to the village resumed and, in 1926/27, six new semi-detached houses were built in Bedford Road. No continuation of the cottage orné style here, but practical modern and handsome villas with generous gardens. In 1930, Dorothy provided the Women's Institute hut for women of the village, situated behind the smithy. Anything needed in the hut was organised by Dorothy, such as Landseer prints for the walls and a large set of china. It was said that the village ladies didn't get a look in.

Richard Shuttleworth (1909–40)

The summer of 1932 saw big celebrations at Old Warden when Richard came into his full inheritance. At a huge party of around 800 tenants, Richard declared that 'friendly relations had always existed between the family and those that lived around, and it was his earnest desire that such a feeling should continue'. Sadly, Richard was squire for just eight years. His tragically short life has been the most well-recorded of all the Squires, and was the inspiration for the direction of the estate after he died.

Richard scraped through his early education, and here there are striking parallels with the 3rd Lord Ongley. Both lost their fathers at a young age, both were unsuited for academia and both were sent to school at Rottingdean. The Revd Dr Hooker's school, which Ongley attended, evolved into St Aubyn's School, where Richard's uncle, Robert Charles Vaughan Lang, became headmaster in 1919, the same year Richard arrived.

Another uncle, Arthur Lang, was a master at the school and in Dorothy Shuttleworth's reminiscences of Richard's life, she commented that,

> He did not fit well into a class, he was too volatile and not interested. His interests were not connected with school life, but mainly with his own home, to which he was devoted. The letters [sent home from school] were mainly questions as to what was happening on the Estate.

Dorothy herself considered that 'when he was able to work at what he really liked such as motorcars and racing, flying and mechanical farming, he then showed his real genius'. He had clearly inherited his grandfather Joseph's love for engineering.

In 1922, a special tutor helped Richard through to Eton where he 'spent nearly all his time at the School of Mechanics', but he was finally sent down for experimenting with explosives in a bathtub. In 1927, he joined the supplementary reserve of the 16th Lancers. He learned how to play polo, how to drive and fly, and bought his first De Havilland Moth.

He built a grass airfield off Hill Lane, where the legacies and passions of two Old Warden squires sit side by side; Lord Ongley's Swiss Garden and Richard Shuttleworth's aerodrome are an unlikely pairing, presenting a striking contrast between the serenity of one and the bustle and noise of the other.

Richard's life was taken up with finding and rebuilding veteran cars, aeroplanes and bicycles, motor and aeroplane racing, hunting, steeplechasing and point-to-pointing, and, as if this wasn't enough, his duties as county councillor and managing his estate.

In 1933, Richard flew a Comper Swift solo for 6,000 miles to Delhi, India, which took thirteen days, in order to take part in an air race for the Viceroy's Cup. Sadly, he had to give up before the start. In 1935, he won the first Donington Grand Prix driving his Alfa Romeo. A press report declared 'young Squire Shuttleworth brought honour to his village of Old Warden, Bedfordshire today when he won the first Grand Prix road race ever held in England'.

Richard had numerous motor and flying accidents, and occasional brushes with the law for speeding and motoring infringements. But, as his close friend, Jimmy Edmunds, wrote 'One has to remember that motoring in the late 1920s and '30s was vastly different from road conditions today', and Edmunds did not remember Richard ever injuring anyone on the road.

In Old Warden, concerns were raised by villagers to the parish council about cars speeding through the village. As a result, in 1936, an attempt was made to impose a speed restriction. Richard was approached for his views and the council minutes later recorded,

Richard Shuttleworth.

A letter was read from Mr Shuttleworth regarding the suggested speed limit through the village, and Mr Goodhand proposed, Mr Cooper seconded that the secretary write to Mr Shuttleworth and make another appeal regarding same.

Richard was clearly unimpressed, and no further mention of speed limits appeared in the council minutes.

Jimmy Edmunds recalled how Richard had much sympathy for his tenants, and would go to great trouble if anyone was unhappy or in need. One day, a little old man turned up to beg a pair of wheels from Richard, as he was no longer strong enough to lift sacks of potatoes off his land. Richard told him he'd see what he could do, and before long hadn't just found some wheels but built the man a cart.

Richard was admired and respected by his tenants, his racing around the farm tracks and terror of his passengers now remembered with a smile by the few left to tell these tales. The estate painter and decorator, Joe Rowe, came to the village in 1911 aged sixteen. Of Richard he recalled that,

> He was a fine gentleman, he used to work the same as everyone else, of course he was an engineer really but he would buckle in and help if he came by and saw you were a bit hard pressed and would take his coat off and help ... there was nothing artificial about him.

Joe also recalled Richard ordering estate workers to remove all the ivy from the cottages, the church, and trees in the Warren, as he'd discovered how much damage it caused. The estate workers were pleased to be kept busy with the remedial work.

His mother recorded that in 1938/39, after his serious racing accident in South Africa, Richard devoted himself to the farms and estate. He invested in new agricultural

Ivy-clad cottages, Nos 34 & 35, The Village (The Shuttleworth Trust).

machinery, including experimenting with a Clayton & Shuttleworth combine harvester by attaching lights to a diesel tractor to enable night-time ploughing. His growing interest in agriculture and forestry was reflected by his election as president of the Beds Agricultural Society. In the village, he converted the Hare & Hounds stables at the Clock House into the new village shop and post office.

For such a daredevil personality, the advent of the Second World War and the need for skilled pilots proved fateful. Richard was tragically killed on night flying practice from RAF Benson, Oxfordshire, on 2 August 1940, when his plane, a Fairey Battle, crashed into a hillside. Just three days later, he was to have been posted to a safer role at the Engineering Branch, to make use of his mechanical skills in investigating air accidents.

Richard never married, and his family complained that he would not join in society parties where he could meet eligible women. There was never any knowledge of a girlfriend, but Dorothy's chauffeur, Charles Clarke, was certain that Richard would have married eventually, and confided to his family that if Richard had fallen for a village girl then he would have married a village girl. Status and place in society meant little to him.

Obituaries described Richard as one of the best known airmen and motor-racing drivers in the country. Adm. Sir Lionel Halsey, who knew Richard well, wrote,

> I knew him ... when he was a mere boy and a real boy he has remained in many ways, in that everything he put his hand to was a delight to him and he took everything up with boyish zest ... He was an indefatigable worker ... I mean a real labourer, who knew no such thing as ending work because the sun went down ... if the job was not done. Those with whom he worked ... would willingly carry on with him, such was his magnetic influence.

Richard's funeral, 1940, Aubrey Pearce leading the horse (Bedfordshire and Luton Archives).

Dorothy Shuttleworth, (1940–68)

Richard's loss was devastating to family, friends and tenants alike, and Dorothy's faith and stoicism shines through in a letter she sent to Richard's engineering friend, A. E. Grimmer of Ampthill:

> I know words fail as you say, but we must always think he is still rushing about doing all the things he loved. He was the best and dearest son, so gallant and brave. I know he has gone straight into life and is in very noble company. It's lovely to feel how beloved he was, and show how blessed I was.

After she was first widowed, Dorothy threw herself into the First World War effort, and she did the same in the Second World War following her son's death. In October 1940, she again allowed the Red Cross to take over part of the house as a ninety-six bed convalescent home, this time taking the role of commandant herself.

Richard left everything to his mother, and she embarked on perpetuating his memory by building a small chapel in the house, which was used by the nurses and convalescing soldiers during the war and later college students. In 1948, Richard's Crescent in Bedford Road was built and consisted of three modern detached houses designed by Dorothy's friend, leading architect Professor Sir Albert Richardson. In 1952, Richardson also designed a new entrance porch to the church dedicated to Richard's memory.

Dorothy wrote a small book, *Richard Ormonde Shuttleworth, Reminiscences of his Life by his Mother*. Bound in Richard's favourite colour – blue – a copy, together with a photograph of Richard, was given to each estate tenant.

But Dorothy's greatest act of memory was to found the Richard Ormonde Shuttleworth Remembrance Trust on 7 May 1946, which remains in existence. In July 1944, she held a meeting of all the estate tenants and told them she was

> giving back all the property and money to the memory of the family who loved the place ... in the form of a trust for a college. We shall take boys leaving school and train them in the science of aviation, agriculture and forestry, both in research and practical work.

The college flourished and Dorothy was awarded an OBE for services to agricultural education in 1963.

She also decided that she wanted a museum in Old Warden to house Richard's cars and aeroplanes. This was eventually opened in 1963, and is now the world-famous Shuttleworth Collection.

Although a trust now owned the village, Dorothy continued to oversee its welfare and preservation which was still very important to her. In the eyes of villagers, she was their figurehead right until her death. If Richard was the last squire, then his indomitable and respected mother, the vicar's daughter, was truly Old Warden's last lady of the manor, and her passing marked the end of the era of the squires.

Richard's Crescent under construction (Bedfordshire and Luton Archives).

3

Tenants

Seven Compact Farms, with comfortable farmhouses and extensive homesteads in the occupation of a highly respectable tenantry of long standing ... Numerous cottages and gardens in the village of Old Warden ... in the occupation of a respectable class of peasantry, at very low rents.

Estate Sale Catalogue, 1872

Representing the tenants in this haunting picture is William Johnson Neal, aged ninety-five. Born in Old Warden of a local farming family, he was tenant farmer at Sweetbriar for all his working life. His picture was taken in 1902 to celebrate his great age. He died a few months later. What tales he could have told. He sits outside his Church End cottage, where he was cared for by a servant (*above opposite*).

And here are the descendants of a long line of peasantry, mother and son, Mary Ann (née Wells) and George Marston, pictured at No. 18 The Village just after the First World War (*below opposite*).

Records of occupations are few in the eighteenth century, but parish registers provide some details listing a blacksmith, gardener, carpenter, dairyman, bricklayer and mason. John Smith was a 'hemp-dresser' around 1700. Hemp could be made into rope or coarse cloth, with workers using a hackle (fine comb) to separate out the coarse part of the hemp. In 1701, John Woodstock was 'the miller', and was probably associated with Doolittle Mill, which now only exists in the barely remembered name of the Hill Lane Bridge, over the stream at the back of the airfield. In 1720, probate was made on the will of a sadler, John Wynde.

In 1788, the Bedford Charity (Harpur Trust) sponsored William Summerfield's seven-year apprenticeship to Joseph Billin, blacksmith, and later, in 1807, a female apprentice was sent to Richard Haines, a mantua (a ladies overdress) maker. Benjamin Briggs, a tailor, appears in 1799.

There are a number of yeomen – small farmers who owned or rented their own land – who gradually became tenant farmers as enclosure placed land ownership with fewer individuals. Occupations for the common labourer (peasantry) revolved around farming – arable, livestock and market gardening. The essential skilled trades were blacksmith, carpenter and shoemaker, but no wheelwright or thatcher is found in the records. There is evidence that the Chambers family of thatchers, from Southill, worked in Old Warden. Over at the hamlet of Hill, closer to Biggleswade, there was a hawker of sweetmeats and a huckster (door-to-door salesman).

William Johnson Neal, 1902
(The Shuttleworth Trust).

Mary Ann and George Marston, *c.* 1920.

Occasionally someone broke the norm, such as Samuel Lawrence Taylor (1813–68) of Claypits Farm. Taylor worked as an inventor from a young age, patenting a new type of plough in 1840 with Shefford iron founders John Sanders and William Williams. His harrow was a prizewinner, gaining a medal at the 1851 Great Exhibition.

There is a consistent pattern of the son following their father's occupation, such as the Dickens family of bricklayers. Dickens the mason repaired the vicarage in 1774, and Daniel Dickens appears in the parish registers in the 1790s described as 'bricklayer and mason'. His son, also Daniel, carried on the business in Old Warden, undoubtedly working for Ongley in his village makeover and the creation of Swiss Garden. There was a whole dynasty of Dickens builders in the area, and the Old Warden family started to diversify towards the 1870s, when David Dickins became a market gardener at Laundry Farm, working 13 acres and employing two men.

Dorothy Shuttleworth wrote in her memoir of Swiss Garden that

> The gates and the railings connecting them to Swiss Garden were made by a wonderful blacksmith who lived in Old Warden. He was Hart and was supposed to be the uncle of Emma Hart, Lady Hamilton.

She was writing about James Hart (1776–1836), the village blacksmith. His supposed relationship to Lady Hamilton was purely gossip, but the gates and railings are the beautiful woodland gate and screen, and the servants' gate dated around 1830. A recent Buildings and Structures Heritage Appraisal of Swiss Garden (Christopher Garrand Consultancy, 2012) stated that they were 'fabricated entirely of wrought iron … by way of high-quality traditional forging and jointing, a considerable technical achievement … the work is probably that of a skilled local blacksmith' (*below*).

James Hart served a seven-year apprenticeship with blacksmith George Larkin of Biggleswade from 1790, having been sponsored by the Bedford Charity. After his marriage

Swiss Garden woodland gate and screen.

in 1810, he settled in Old Warden. In 1822, his first child, Ann, made a wonderful needlework picture of the Vicarage House (*see Chapter 5*).

Hart had nine children, John (1818–83) who carried on the family business in Old Warden. Two other sons were blacksmiths, James Jnr, a farm smith at Park Farm, Woburn, who later purchased the smithy at Cople, and Thomas who went to Northampton as a blacksmith, probably to work in one of the large foundries. Another son, Robert, also went to Northampton to learn the skills of a cobbler, later returning to Old Warden.

James and John Hart's blacksmiths shop was located at Parsonage Piece, but, with Joseph Shuttleworth's remodelling of the nearby park entrance, such industry would have been out of place, and the building materials were sold at auction in April 1875:

> Capital hovel and lean-to standing in Blacksmith's Close, near the Warden Lodge, the blacksmith's shop and shoeing shed, brew house, stable, and a cottage; also a good barn and pigsty, as standing in Warden village, in the occupation of Mr John Hart and Mrs Sears.

A new smithy was built at the rear of No. 32 The Village and is now a private house. Seventy years of accessible census records provide an overview of life and work in the parish, from the accession of Victoria to the eve of the First World War. Population figures are revealing. The estimated population of '*Wardone*' in Domesday was 100, and the population in 2011 was 330, showing limited growth over 900 years. In the early eighteenth century, returns to the Bishop of Lincoln show between forty and sixty-eight families; around 160 to 270 inhabitants. At its nineteenth-century peak, in 1821, there were 670 inhabitants. From 1860 onwards, the population gradually decreased; by 1911 it stood at 406.

The mechanisation of agriculture, growth of towns and industry, ease of mobility and changes in occupations all account for this change. A good example is the family of John and Mary Ann Marston, with nine children born between 1843 and 1866. By the time they were adults, only three had remained in the parish. One became a cemetery caretaker in Tavistock, Devon, two moved around the country for work in agriculture and industry, and one joined the Coldstream Guards. He later settled with his two sisters and their husbands in East Ardsley, Yorkshire, all living within a few streets of each other, where work was found on the area's railways, quarries, mills and mines.

The census offers few surprises, with agricultural work predominating throughout, particularly straw-plaiting from the 1850s to 1880s, with just one plaiter remaining by 1891. A young jockey, Charles Nott (aged fifteen), appears in 1851, and no doubt linked to the Ongley passion for horseracing.

Some women held responsible occupations; many farmers' widows took at least nominal charge of the business with their sons' support. In 1859, Susannah Whitteridge of Abbey Farm succeeded her husband both as farmer and overseer of the poor. Sarah Sear was a dairy woman, holding grazing land for her dairy cattle. After blacksmith James Hart died, his widow, Kitty, entered blacksmith as her census occupation, probably running the business while her son worked the forge. A midwife appears in 1851, the elderly Elizabeth Garner, and Sarah Street of Secots Hill (Bedford Road) was running a grocer's by the early 1860s, her husband working on the land. Women were also dressmakers and bonnet-makers, milliners and needlewomen.

By 1861, the nearby Midland Railway provided some work; a railway servant was resident in the village and a few platelayers (men who patrolled the railway track) appear from 1871.

In the Tunnel area was a dwelling called the Brickyard, and a brickworks and clay mill is shown here on the 1880s Ordnance Survey map. In 1871, John Gambril, William Thompson and his son, all brick makers, lived here. The Gambril and Thompson families and John Willsher were still making bricks into the 1880s.

More modern trades arrived in the 1880s and 1890s such as house decorator, electrical engineer, plumber and glazier, engine driver, letter carrier, postmistress and sub-postmaster. Richard Geal was a portable engine driver and Joseph Scott was the rural postman. In 1911, there was still one lacemaker – young Clara Pearce – and a midwife, Mary Ann Ward, a cobbler and a blacksmith – Charles Goodhand of No. 34 The Village, whose forge eventually fell silent in the 1920s. There were also four electrical engineers, apprentice plumbers, an accountant, an engine fitter and two shop assistants.

The Nottingham family provided decades of shepherds. In 1809, John Nottingham, Ongley's shepherd, won a prize for raising 550 lambs from 500 ewes. In 1938, Charles Nottingham died aged seventy-six, having worked for the Woodwards of Abbey Farm for sixty years. His sister, Lucy, was a devoted general servant to the Woodwards all her life, a fact commemorated on her gravestone.

Loyalty and long service abounded. David Ward (1818–95) was thoughtfully laid to rest under a yew tree, his memorial telling his story:

> For fifty years woodman on the Old Warden Estate
> As the tree falls so must it lie
> As the man lives; so will he die
> As the man dies, so must he be
> All through the days of eternity
> This stone was placed by Caroline Shuttleworth in token of her esteem and regard for a
> worthy and God fearing couple and as a memorial of long and faithful service

The Sawmill in the Warren was once a thriving scene of activity with an engine shed, timber sheds and tool shed. Now there is no trace of these buildings, the last pantiled sheds being removed recently. The sawpit measured 42 feet 6 inches by 22 feet, in which the 'under-dog' and 'top-dog' sawed lengths of timber before steam-power took over.

Joseph Scott (1843–1914), of No. 49 Old Warden, received the Imperial Service Medal in 1908 for his thirty-five years of service as rural postman for Northill, Old Warden and Southill. His retirement was celebrated with gifts from each of the villages, and the press estimated he had travelled 200,000 miles during his career.

In 1844, Old Warden gained a full postal service with the support of William Henry Whitbread. A rural messenger was initially appointed at 12s per week, and the first sub post office was opened in 1873 at Parsonage Piece, where William King was the village grocer and letter receiver. William Mayes took over in the 1890s. There were two deliveries and collections daily.

The first public telephone in the village was placed in the porch of No. 46 The Village next to Jacob's Well. The remains of where the brackets were are still visible. This was the

The Sawmill, 1898.

Joseph Scott, rural postman, 1898.

house of Billy Newton, an estate clerk, who may have heard some interesting conversations from behind his front door. A red telephone box was later placed discreetly in bushes near the schoolhouse. It was said that Mrs Shuttleworth did not want such modernity spoiling the setting of her village.

Bridging the gap between squires, vicar, farmers and peasantry was the steward who ran the estate. Three generations of the Reynolds family served the 2nd Lord Ongley, through to Joseph Shuttleworth. Matthew Reynolds (1811–88) of the 2nd generation was a skilled surveyor, making tithe valuation maps for three districts of Bedfordshire, with another five attributed as his work. Two of his tithe maps are held at the National Archives, Radwell, Herts (1837) – described as a first-class map – and Old Warden (1849).

At the time of the great Victorian railways' construction, Reynolds represented Ongley's interests at inquiries and select committees where building was proposed on his land. His experience made him an expert witness in such matters as assessing land rates and values.

Reynolds lived at Beech Cottage (now the Old Vicarage) and he was also a farmer, renting 420 acres in Old Warden Park and employing thirteen men and three boys. He was chair of the parish vestry and a churchwarden and, at the time of his death, was vice chairman of member of the Board of Guardians of Biggleswade Union Workhouse.

His son, George Matthew Reynolds (1845–83), was also a surveyor and auctioneer, working for both Ongley and Shuttleworth, and running auctions for Joseph Shuttleworth when he was reshaping the estate. But the family fortunes were fading. After a brush with bankruptcy, George died aged just thirty-eight and thus ended the Reynolds' dynasty in the village.

Richard Shuttleworth's land agent, William Fellowes, went on to greater things – in 1936 the King appointed him agent for the Sandringham estate. Fellowes was succeeded

Beech Cottage, now The Old Vicarage.

by Lt.-Col Leonard Wyndham Diggle, who purchased the former Vicarage House in 1937, renaming it Orchard Grange.

Another distinguished tenant and national figure was Adm. Sir Lionel Halsey (1872–1949). He came to Old Warden in 1919, settling at Mount Pleasant House with wife Morwenna, and daughters, Joan and Ruth. His brother Walter's firm were solicitors to the Shuttleworth family. Known simply as 'the Admiral' to villagers, his presence placed him as a wonderful role model to young Richard Shuttleworth and support to the village during the Second World War.

He had a brilliant career in the Royal Navy, commanding a battery of naval guns at the defence of Ladysmith in South Africa. During the First World War, he commanded a ship at the Battles of Heligoland, and Dogger Bank. After the war, he was appointed Chief of Staff to the Prince of Wales (the future King Edward VIII) for his 1919 tour of Canada, USA, Australia and New Zealand for which Halsey received the KCVO and GCVO.

In 1920, he was appointed comptroller and treasurer to the Prince of Wales, and became a royal equerry in 1921. By 1926, he had risen to the rank of admiral. He can often be glimpsed in television footage of the Prince of Wales. He was strongly opposed to the Prince's relationship with Wallis Simpson and, in 1936, was not given a role in the new King's household. After the abdication, he found favour with George VI and became an extra equerry and keeper of the Jewel House.

In keeping with his life of service to his country, he played a major role in the Second World War as county director of the British Red Cross and member of the Home Guard. Locally, he was on Old Warden's Second World War Invasion Committee, found time to visit the school to talk to the children, and, together with Lady Halsey, supported local fundraising events.

Above left: Adm. Sir Lionel Halsey and Lady Halsey.

Above right: Mount Pleasant, the Admiral's aviary to the left of the house.

4

Servants

Every Sunday, Mrs Waby the housekeeper, marched the housemaids to church through the park and village, the girls under strict instruction not to look to left or right. The village lads took great delight in trying to catch the eye of a housemaid, offering suitable words of encouragement along the route!

George Marston's tale of the Shuttleworth housekeeper *c.* 1910

Clustered around the Ongley mausoleum are many old and decaying gravestones, the burials having taken place from the late eighteenth century onward. The Ongleys liked their favoured servants laid to rest close by; this was not unique, as a walk in Southill churchyard reveals the Whitbreads did the same.

We find head gardener, James Beagarie and his wife, schoolmistress Bethalina, Ongley Stewards Edward Jackson and Andrew Lain. The latter 'lived fifty-one years in the family of the late and present Lord', and was the grand age of ninety-one when he died in 1811. George Ongley's stud groom, Thomas Morgan, who was with Frederick Ongley when he died, and another groom, William Proverbs, are both buried here.

Fanny Woodley and Elizabeth Ross are buried alongside the Stewards. Both women were of independent means in the last years of their lives, likely in receipt of the annuities which Ongley generously provided. Elizabeth Ross was a 'former nurse' – possibly nursemaid to the last Ongley children. She lived in the village at Pleasant Place, the earlier name for Swiss Cottage, a prestigious home for a favoured servant.

Also near to the mausoleum are the graves of some of the large Dickens family of bricklayers, and all three generations of the Reynolds family.

Sometimes the relationship between master and servant soured, as a court case against the 3rd Lord Ongley reveals.

In 1860, Mr J. Thomas, Ongley's former horse dealer, petitioned the Court of Common Pleas to recover five years arrears of a £100 annuity allegedly owed to him by Ongley. The annuity had been secured on a bond of £2,000, given for services as stud groom and confidential servant to Ongley from 1824–33. Ongley claimed that Thomas was perpetrating a fraud, and it's clear that Thomas was probably trying to blackmail Ongley, using the threat of revealing 'affectionate' letters sent to him by Ongley.

Ongley's mother apparently disliked Thomas, and objected to him working for her son, so Ongley set him up as his London horse dealer with a stable in Oxford Street, giving him the bond and annuity.

In 1846, Thomas asked Ongley for a lump sum of £1,000 in lieu of the annuity so he could buy a small pub in Wales; he was then without work and living with friends. Ongley paid him £1,000 in cash but did not get a receipt, and when given the surrendered bond threw it in a fire to destroy it. Ongley admitted in his evidence that he was not much of a business man, failed to read and understand the bond and did not get his solicitor to examine it. During the hearing it transpired that Ongley had written letters to Thomas starting 'My dear boy', and he treated Thomas as a friend more than a servant. Thomas threatened to reveal the letters but Ongley was well advised, and produced an offensive letter sent to him from Thomas, which sought money with implied threats. Thomas, Ongley said, had harassed him for money over the years, and this is why he stopped paying the annuity.

In the end, Thomas's solicitor withdrew the case having not been aware that Ongley had letters in evidence against his client, and the case concluded with an order that all letters be impounded. The friendship with an unscrupulous servant had gone badly wrong.

A coyly worded newspaper report of 1848, titled 'A Schoolmaster's Blunder', tells the story of a feisty servant girl and a rather naughty village schoolmaster. The schoolmaster was 'walking a lonely path' in the park when he met the female servant of Lord Ongley's steward. He behaved rudely to the girl by 'trespassing on his own modesty' (in modern terms a 'flasher'). She defended herself by knocking a pitcher she had in her hand about the 'intruder's bump of vanity', breaking the pitcher in the process, but it did the trick, as the miscreant made a hasty retreat. On hearing the sorry tale the next morning, the girl's employer, probably steward Matthew Reynolds, gave the schoolmaster a sound horsewhipping, 'as, no doubt, the powers of his memory will call into perpetual remembrance'. This lowly servant girl had been believed and supported, and the schoolmaster was disgraced.

When the last Lord Ongley died in 1877, in the 3rd carriage of the funeral cortège was Thomas Wheatley, described as the long and faithful servant of Lord Ongley.

Born in Old Warden in 1833, Wheatley was one of seven children of an agricultural labourer. Rather than working on the land, he decided to leave the village and find his luck in London by going into service. By 1850, Wheatley was employed as the lowly page of an earl's widowed daughter in Belgravia. He must have quickly learnt the skills to prepare him to move up the 'downstairs' ladder, for within the next ten years the village lad became Lord Ongley's butler.

Wheatley worked alongside housekeeper, Ann Martin, both remaining with Ongley to his death, and in the spring of 1877, very shortly after the funeral, Wheatley married Virtue Martin, Ann's sister.

In his will, Ongley left Wheatley his three dogs to care for and also,

> My pony chair, pony and harness, my gun, all my wardrobe and rugs, the furniture in the housekeepers room, the musical clock in the library, and the furniture belonging to me which at the time of my decease shall be in the cottage at Old Warden occupied by his [Wheatley's] mother.

Ann Martin was given all of the furniture in Ongley's servant's hall at Bushey Lodge, his kitchen utensils and his common dinner service. Both were also left sizeable legacies, with £3,550 to Wheatley and £1,750 to Ann Martin. A comfortable retirement now beckoned and Thomas, Virtue and Ann moved to Rose Cottage in Whittlesey, the former butler and housekeeper now well able to afford the services of their own domestic servant.

The Swiss Cottage in Swiss Garden was used from the 1840s and 1850s by house servants. In 1841, Mary Nind, aged seventy-three, and domestic servant Eliza Barnes, aged nineteen, lived in one part with young gardener William Roberts in the other. In the 1850s, Hannah Palliser, a widow of fifty-eight, lived in the cottage describing herself as 'keeper of Swiss Cottage' in the census. Her death notice in the *North London News* of 3 December 1864 records her as 'a nobleman's faithful domestic', and that she 'For some time had received an annuity from Lord Ongley. It appears that the deceased resided for some time in a lodge attached to his lordship's mansion near Biggleswade.'

The female servants may have kept the garden buildings clean and tidy, possibly prepared refreshments and even cared for the exotic birds in the aviary.

Just as it is difficult to imagine living in Swiss Garden, another Ongley building, Queen Anne's Summerhouse, was also occupied at this time. John Stonebridge (1804–85) was head gamekeeper and lived in Queen Anne's with his large family for around forty years, possibly from his marriage in the late 1820s. By the 1840s, ten people lived in the summer house, Stonebridge, his wife and their eight children – Sarah Stonebridge had a child almost every year.

How did this family live in a building constructed as a folly or hunting lodge? The basement housed a fireplace, and there was a well for water nearby shared with Squirrels Cottage. Just five of the family were in occupation in 1871, when Stonebridge was still active as gamekeeper. He retired to a house in Broom and died aged eighty-one, surviving his wife, Sarah, by five years. They are buried at All Saints, Southill. Lord Ongley had

Queen Anne's summer house.

clearly held Stonebridge in high esteem, for among the legacies left to Old Warden people was a sum of £50 'to my late gamekeeper, Stonebridge'.

Reflecting the Ongley practice, the long-serving Shuttleworth butler John Bardsley Hunt (1836–1916) and housekeeper Ann Waby (1843–1918) are buried next to each other in front of the Shuttleworth family grave. Their gravestones, now sadly decayed and nearly illegible, were erected by Richard and Dorothy Shuttleworth, the inscription describing them as servants and friends of three generations of the Shuttleworth family, Joseph, Frank and Richard.

At Richard's christening in 1909, Frank Shuttleworth's speech made special mention of a present from 'two old servants who had fifty years of uninterrupted service in his family (butler and housekeeper)'. Hunt and Waby were both born in Lincolnshire and had worked at Hartsholme for Joseph Shuttleworth – Hunt as butler and Waby initially as cook – before coming to Old Warden sometime after the new mansion was built.

The photograph of Hunt (*centre*), with two footmen, was taken at Scarborough when the family were probably staying with Alfred Shuttleworth at his summer residence, Red Court.

The Shuttleworths employed a wide range of servants. On census day 1911, the family were at their house in Berkeley Square with young Richard, and here they were cared for by a valet, ladies' maid, cook/housekeeper, children's nurse and a nursemaid, two housemaids and a kitchen maid. Remaining at Old Warden were the butler, housekeeper and two footmen, a hall boy, cook, five domestic housemaids, two kitchen maids, a scullery maid and a domestic nurse. Twenty-three staff in total, not counting the grooms, coachmen, gardeners and laundry-maids.

During the Ongley period, Laundry Farm, Bedford Road, had been the Glebe (or Vicarage) Farm that belonged to the church. The name changed after Joseph Shuttleworth bought it and decided to create a laundry here to service his new house. This newspaper advert appeared in 1900:

John Hunt and two footmen (John Newton Collection, Manchester Archives).

Housemaids and gardener George Marston at Mount Pleasant, early 1920s.

Wanted, for cottage laundry (unfurnished), a thorough practical laundress, to undertake the laundry work of Old Warden Park, including nine female servants. Married. Husband to work upon the estate. The laundry, with good cottage and garden attached is fitted up with the requisites of the latest designs.

The successful applicant was Emma Fox, a widow in her fifties who had three children of working age. Ernest described as a 'car man', Rose working with her mother as laundry maid and Marmaduke who was a young groom. Another young girl lived with them, acting as both servant and laundry maid. By 1911, there were four laundry maids living at The Laundry, aged from twenty to thirty-five.

No country house could run without men to manage the horses. William John Foster came to Old Warden in 1890, as coachman and groom to Frank Shuttleworth. Frank had specially asked Foster to move to Old Warden to work for him, having known him as stud groom and huntsman to the Cambridgeshire Hunt when Frank was master of foxhounds.

The family lived at Lakeside Cottage. In 1932 at the age of seventy-seven, a broken leg put paid to Foster's continued employment and he died a few years later. The Foster family stayed in the village, his son Douglas and later his grandson, Bill, market gardening at Laundry Farm.

In 1899, tragedy was to strike one of the Shuttleworth grooms. Travers Francis and his wife, Eleanor, lived in Main Lodge, the village entrance to the park. The press reported the circumstances under the heading 'An Extraordinary case from Bedford':

Deceased was a stud groom in the employ of Maj. Shuttleworth ... on 29 August he was exercising some hunters when one of them shied and kicked him in the leg. He was able to ride back to the stables ... and Maj. Shuttleworth took him to his home. His wife then fetched Dr Winckworth from Shefford who was of the opinion the leg was not broken. He had lost a lot of blood and was put to bed for a week, all of which time he was in fearful agony ... he then went to Bedford Infirmary where Dr Ross at once found he had a compound fracture of the leg.

William Foster.

An operation was performed to remove loose pieces of bone and Francis was able to walk when he eventually left the infirmary on 19 November. He had to be readmitted on 4 March the following year, when shivering fits showed he was absorbing poison from the original wound. Septicaemia had set in. Despite every effort to save him, he died on 29 March. His widow told the inquest that in her view her husband could have been saved had he been sent to the infirmary immediately, but the verdict was accidental death. Poor Eleanor returned to live with her elderly parents in Cople, supporting herself by working with her mother as a lacemaker.

The chauffeur/gardener to Admiral Halsey at Mount Pleasant was the First World War veteran George Marston, who worked for the Halseys for forty years. George had the privilege of driving the Admiral and the Prince of Wales to the R101 disaster funeral at Cardington, in 1930.

Another chauffeur was Charles Clarke, who came to work for Dorothy and Richard Shuttleworth in 1934, having been previously employed in Harrold by the Master of the Oakley Hunt, Captain Arkwright.

Around the early 1930s, Miss Helen Willett came to teach Richard Shuttleworth how to play the violin. Quite how the engine-mad Richard took to the violin is not known, but the family certainly took to Miss Willett as she never left. Her family lived in Bedford, and she had an older sister called Margaret who was a trained nurse. During the Second World War, the Willett sisters were to play important roles in the Red Cross Convalescent Home.

Miss Willett became Dorothy Shuttleworth's companion and secretary, fiercely guarding both her mistress and her finances. Mrs Shuttleworth was so fond of the Willetts' that she had a house built for them on the edge of the village near the Swiss Garden – Colemoreham.

In 1963, an eighteen-year-old St Helenian, Cyril Thomas, embarked on a 5,000-mile journey that would change his life. He was to be the last Shuttleworth footman and chauffeur, serving Dorothy for the last five years of her life. Raised by his grandparents

Charles Clarke at Old Warden Park.

and uncle, with his father in the British Army, Cyril decided to take his chance by enrolling in an agency that arranged jobs for domestic servants in the UK. Arriving by ship at Southampton, Cyril was shocked by his first encounter with the freezing British weather, and waiting for him at the quayside was the father he had never seen.

On arrival at Old Warden, Cyril still remembers the cold and that he had no suitable clothing for such weather. His first night was in the unwelcoming Bothy, and his first meal was sausage and mash.

Miss Willett and the matron decided which of the new arrivals would work in the kitchens, and who would be trained to work directly for Mrs Shuttleworth. Cyril fervently hoped for the kitchens, but was chosen to be introduced to Mrs Shuttleworth. She was kind to him; she got her London butler to train him in the duties of footman and provided his uniform. He learnt how to approach people, to clean silver, decant wine and put out sherry and cigarettes (Senior Service) for guests. He also became the only man allowed into Dorothy's bedroom when he served her breakfast.

After a couple of years, Cyril felt stifled and wanted to move on, but, after searching questions from Mrs Shuttleworth as to his reasons, she offered him the additional role of chauffeur and he was taught to drive. Cyril felt compelled to stay; such kindness could not be ignored.

As well as Cyril and Miss Willett there was the cook, Mrs Vintner, Glad Jenkins the housekeeper, Hilda Smith the seamstress and Mr Bull the odd-job man. In the last two years of Mrs Shuttleworth's life, she also had a lady's maid, Miss Hill.

After fifty years working and living in Old Warden, Cyril retains fond memories of Mrs Shuttleworth and her family, and is a last reminder of the lost world of domestic service to the squires in the big house.

5

Children and Education

Upon view the body of Ann Page, aged five years, who ... being left in a room by her mother whilst she was gone to pick up deadwood, by some accident the child's clothes caught fire, and upon the mother's return she found her daughter in the middle of the room with her clothes on fire, and nearly consumed ... she died in about two hours.

Coroners report, Old Warden, 10 December 1825

As the weather is so severe just now and so many of the lesser children cry of cold, I shall limit recreation to 5 minutes and dismiss at 11.50.

School Log Book entry, 22 November 1891

Child tragedies were common, and the only known murder in Old Warden during this period was that of a child, in 1931. This most shocking tragedy befell the Milton family. George Milton was a horse keeper, married to Frenchwoman Bertha Maria. They had a ten-year-old daughter, Violette.

One Saturday, Bertha took Violette out for a walk to pick wild flowers. They never returned home. George called the police, a search by lamplight began and later that evening two bodies were found in a deep pool, around 1 mile from the village. They had drowned, tied together by a scarf. Bertha left a suicide note in a basket hanging on a bush by the pool. It said 'I cannot bear this suffering any longer, but I don't want to leave Violette by herself. I am very sorry to do this, for you have been a good husband.'

George reported at the inquest that the marriage had been happy, but his wife had suffered from severe head pains. With his evidence and Bertha's note, a verdict of murder and suicide was recorded. The site of the pool was not identified, although the ancient fish pond near Manor Farm on the Bedford Road/Rowney Lane junction fits the description.

Life dealt blows to the young in various guises. A risk of early death, if not from the array of common illnesses, could be a child playing too close to an open fire. As well as poor Ann Page, an inquest from 1840 tells of Lucy Wells, aged nearly three, playing near the grate when her clothes caught fire and the flames couldn't be put out in time. Lucy died the following day. A number of children were reported as having been killed by lightning strikes. In 1933, Horace Bowles of Sweetbriar Cottages was out tending sheep in a thunderstorm. Running for shelter, he was struck and killed. In 1916, Walter Rook, the eight-year-old son of a Kings Hill horse-keeper, was hailed a hero when he attempted to stop a runaway farm horse and was killed in the process.

Ann Hart Needlework Picture, 1822 (The Higgins).

But there are happier tales of children's lives in the village, and young Ann Hart left us a little treasure.

Ann Hart (1811–75), the eldest daughter of Old Warden's blacksmith James Hart, worked her picture when just eleven years old and the Orchard Grange of today is instantly recognised. She depicted what she saw – birds, animals, trees, flowers – and the people she knew, undoubtedly Revd Neve's family who were then resident at the vicarage. Close inspection reveals red squirrels (greys not yet introduced), a peacock, a horse walking up the carriage drive, and is that really a fancy white dog wearing a coat? One of the girls holds a dog by a lead, another sits by a cow and the lady holding a flower could be the vicar's wife Elizabeth Neve, her dress straight from a Jane Austen adaptation.

When Revd Neve died in 1843, his household goods were listed for auction, including his Alderney cows which were brown and white, just as shown in Ann's picture. The auction notice also listed 'the greenhouse, comprising all the glazed roof, sashes, doors etc; garden pots, orange trees and a variety of choice plants'. Was this the large conservatory attached to the house?

The Hart family most probably lived at Parsonage Piece, as the blacksmith's was also situated here. Ann was a similar age to Emily and Frances Neve, they might have played and were taught needlework together. Ann went on to marry village cobbler George

Honour Barratt, but after his early death she moved to Clophill upon her second marriage, to carpenter, Joseph Neal.

Ann was lucky to be the daughter of a skilled tradesman, but other children were less fortunate. Real-life scarecrows kept birds off the fields around Old Warden, using rattles, banging buckets or shouting. The 1861 census records three scarecrows, Joseph Stokes and George Scott, both aged eight, and John Wiltshire, aged nine. George Spring, aged ten, was a twitch gatherer – 'twitch' the common name for couch grass, the bane of today's gardeners.

In 1871, George Burrage, aged nine, was a field keeper, Charles Nottingham, also nine, a farm boy and James Scott, thirteen, a kitchen boy. In 1898, Harold Samuels, aged ten, was absent from school for fifty-five hours because of field keeping, for which he was paid 3s. A field keeper kept birds, pests and other animals off the crops. The 1851 census shows the extent of child labour in Old Warden parish. Seventy-seven children between the ages of four to fourteen were engaged either in agriculture (boys), or the country craft of straw plaiting (girls and some younger boys). The children of the better off, such as tenant farmers and tradesmen, could attend a school, their parents paying a subscription for their lessons. The poorer and larger families, the real peasantry, needed their children to earn some income from an early age simply to survive.

The boy's tasks also included weeding, minding livestock, stone clearing and helping at harvest time. Young scarecrows were expected to be out in the sown fields as long as the birds were feeding, dawn to dusk, and earned just a few pence per day toward the family income, a lonely job seven days a week.

In Bedfordshire, the girls and women in the north of the county were mostly lacemakers, and in the south straw plaiting predominated, the hat-making market of nearby Luton dictating occupations in the villages. Some Old Warden women were lacemakers, but the majority were straw plaiters. The Women's Institute contributed an interesting tale about straw plaiting in their 1949 Yearbook:

> Villagers used to take their straw plait to the saw pit (in the Warren) and let it hang down the pit while working to see who had the longest strip. The plait was made into bundles of 20 yards. It was collected by a Mrs Wells and most of it was sold at Shefford Market.

The Shefford Plait Market was held each Friday in the High Street. Its district of plaiters produced the narrow 'Twist' plait, as well as some 'Devons' or single straw plait.

There was nothing at all unusual in Old Warden's child labourers. Even into the 1960s, very young village children went to the fields with their mothers who were earning 'pin money' by picking peas. Children were often left to play or read at the field edges, and there were many upset stomachs from over indulgence on the deliciously sweet peas. Teenagers from the village also worked for local farmers during their school holidays, emulating their predecessors by potato, pea and bean picking, and pulling weeds such as 'fat hen' from bean fields – not one of the author's fondest memories.

Various Education Acts gradually brought about changes, making education compulsory for children aged five to ten in 1880, but adherence could be patchy. The teaching of straw plaiting in schools was made illegal in the 1870s, and the craft gradually died out with the import of cheaper Chinese, Japanese and Italian Plait. By the early 1900s, there were only a few hundred plaiters in the counties surrounding Luton, compared with around 30,000 in 1871.

The understanding of education in Old Warden in the eighteenth and early nineteenth centuries is limited. Schools came and went, the plait schools may have taught reading or writing, and Sunday schools generally covered these basics.

In 1706, a church visitation records no schools operating in the parish. By 1713, Sir Samuel Ongley was paying for the schooling of one each of William Abbot's and Goody Tavit's children at 2s 6d per quarter, possibly at the 'private' school that existed in 1717. However the visitation of 1720 again states there were no schools in the village. A 1728 terrier (inventory) refers to John Baker, schoolmaster. In 1802, Samuel Whitbread called for a report on education in his locality. In Old Warden 'Bunting' had endowed a school for twelve boys to be taught to read and write, also running a Sunday school for thirty to forty children who were taught to read. A William Bunting was noted in the parish register in 1793 as 'clerk of ye parish'.

An 1818 Select Committee questionnaire reveals a school for seventy children, but only half attended. There was a Sunday school for eighty children and three other village schools, where around fifteen children were taught in each. The 1822 *Glebe Terrier* tells of a school 'recently built in stud clay and tile with a yard belonging', which was at the rear of the clock house and workhouse. In 1876, Joseph Shuttleworth purchased the charity land on which this school was still standing, described as 'for many years used as the parish schoolroom'.

In 1833, a government questionnaire reveals a daily school of thirty-six females (males are missing), a Sunday school of thirty males and forty-five females paid for by two subscribers, and several lace and plait schools for around thirty-five children who were also taught to read, paid for by parents.

A confusing melee of educational establishments is detailed in a Church of England enquiry into church schools in 1846/47. There was an Infants Daily School for thirty boys and forty girls, a Sunday school for fifty boys and seventy girls, Lord Ongley's School of eleven boys and sixteen girls, and two other daily schools for sixteen boys and sixteen girls each. Only two schoolmistresses are recorded in the census of 1841 and 1851.

The 1870 Elementary Education Act made it necessary fovr parishes to provide schooling for children aged five to thirteen. On 2 December 1870, the new school board met to discuss the Act. It was chaired by Henry Browning, who was then renting Warden House from Lord Ongley. The committee consisted of the vicars of Old Warden and Northill, steward and farmer Matthew Reynolds, farmers Neal, Heading, Dillamore, Taylor, Woodward, and Mrs Whitteridge. Unsurprisingly, in this agricultural village, the committee voted to adopt the voluntary system of attendance as opposed to compulsory, no doubt prioritising the contribution the boys made to village labour and family subsistence. The committee could have created a bye-law via Parliament had they wanted to make attendance compulsory in the parish; this option was recorded to be explored in 1878 after complaints were made about attendance by Miss Twysden the mistress, but no record was kept on whether the bye-law was obtained.

Local subscriptions were needed for building the new school and teacher's house. Lord Ongley donated the site and a sum of £100. Samuel Whitbread and Henry Browning gave £50 each, John Harvey of Ickwell £15, Revds Baker and Pott £25 each, and Matthew Reynolds £10. The farmers contributed smaller sums, as did the blacksmith, market gardener, publican and grocer. Overall, the school cost £1,579 with Joseph Shuttleworth providing the rather large shortfall of £1,232 4s 11d.

With Joseph Shuttleworth appearing on the scene in 1872, the board abandoned the original plans of architect W. Watson in favour of Shuttleworth's proposal to use his own architect, Henry Clutton. Clutton was taken along to the managers meeting of October 1872 to produce his plans. By 11 January 1875, the board was able to convene in the new school classroom.

Parents had to contribute the 'school pence', and a levy was made on the parish rates to pay for the material needs of the school. In 1878, the board decided that an equitable system for the weekly school pence levy would be for labourer's families to pay: one child in the family (2d), two children (4d) and three or more children (5d). Tradesmen's children and children of non-labourers were to pay 3d per child.

The new school did not fare too well with its early mistresses. Miss White clashed with Revd J. G. A. Baker in May 1878, and this 'Manager's Minute Book' entry provides intriguing insight into the attitudes of the time:

Mr Baker complained that Miss White had objected to allow three children to leave the school to join a singing class at the church. He also complained that she had used corporal punishment in the school and that she had been to Biggleswade late at night. Miss White stated in justification of children going after 4 o'clock, but could not let them go at 3 o'clock as it interfered with their duties in the school. Mr Baker afterwards came to the school and ordered the children to go, saying he was master and she was to do as he wished. Mr Baker gave her positive orders not to go out after dark and to go to him for orders.

Old Warden School (The Shuttleworth Trust).

Mr Baker the following morning asked her if she would promise not to use corporal punishment again, and she said she could not promise. Mr Baker then asked her if she had better leave if she could not conform to Mr Baker's wishes. The corporal punishment consisted of striking the children on the hand with a pointer and took place after school hours.

Miss White told the board she had been to Biggleswade to take an exam in a science and art class, and she had not travelled home alone. The board was indecisive, deferring any decision until the next meeting when they hoped Joseph Shuttleworth would be there, as the squire's leadership was always needed. Miss White had to apologise for her disrespect towards the vicar and, at the July board meeting, she was dismissed with a month's notice.

Other mistresses came highly recommended, but as soon as school inspections raised issues with performance they were dismissed. Miss Twysden failed to keep control of the boys, but had no problem managing the girls. She was given three months' notice. Miss Warner was found to have 'serious failings of temper' and she resigned. Poor Edwin Capon, who came as schoolmaster in 1887 from Bedford Harpur Boys' School, found himself forced to resign in 1892, the board refusing to give a reason for wanting him gone beyond their decision to seek a new master. He recorded in the school logbook that the news was 'to my great astonishment', and he 'felt thoroughly unfit for work'. Considerable indignant newspaper coverage on Capon's behalf reveals the likely reason for his dismissal – politics. Capon was a Liberal and suspected that he had offended the school committee and the squire by declining a request from Caroline Shuttleworth to canvas for the Tories at the July 1892 general election.

John G. Wall succeeded him, and on the surface all was well until 1919, when school inspections reported a weakness in attainment:

> Six children in Standard One were promoted from the Infant's Division last Easter, but were returned in September. They are at present in a lamentable state of backwardness. This makes the future of the school a matter of grave concern, and it is evident that serious steps will have to be taken to save it from inefficiency.

Wall resigned of his own accord in 1923, but refused to vacate the schoolhouse to allow the new headmistress, Miss Booth, to move in. The school managers sought to evict Wall via the courts. Dorothy Campbell wrote to Mr Whitbread for help saying, 'No-one can apparently get Mr Wall out of the schoolhouse', with some rather more personal thoughts on the matter. Wall moved out before legal process ensued, and Miss Booth did an excellent job in turning the school around.

But what of the children? During Miss Twysden's tenure there is an example of one boy's unruly behaviour:

> The mistress reported to the committee that Burrage had, contrary to her orders, continued to use a sling and had broken a window in the classroom … his elder brother was also guilty of a similar offence last year.

Young Burrage was reprimanded by the chairman and his father, an estate gardener with a large family, was ordered to pay the cost of repairs. It was always the boys. In October 1891,

School class, *c.* 1905. Wall is pictured on the left and schoolmistress Gertrude Endersby is on the far right (John Newton Collection, Manchester Archives).

it was noted that Charles Vintiner was caned for impudence to a junior mistress, and several boys were punished for climbing trees and shrubs during dinner hour. Their toilet facilities also caused a problem, with the inspectors noting in 1896: 'The urinal is not very sweet.'

Good things happened though. In March 1891, Edwin Capon recorded this amusing scene:

> Mrs [Caroline] Shuttleworth and Mr Bourdillon [vicar] came to school and distributed oranges and nuts. This afternoon I gave the children ten minutes play ... during which time the room was swept to free it from nutshells.

The Shuttleworth family, their butler, housekeeper and the vicar regularly visited and gave treats to the children, such as Easter buns and Christmas mince pies. Best of all was the annual Shuttleworth School treat in the park, when school closed for the day.

There was a constant battle with absenteeism, with boys labouring in the fields and girls sometimes kept away to tend younger siblings if the mother was ill:

6 March 1891	Charles Rook away this week at work. Shall report.
	Mr Miller SAC (School Attendance Committee) called and took three names; Charles Rook, Charles Vintiner, F. Wells.
25 March 1891	Percy Marriot, H. Marriott, A. Stacey, G. Marriott kept at home to go mice killing. Last Friday, Percy and his brothers kept at home as it was his birthday.
27 June 1898	Several boys and girls away from school engaged in picking peas.

4 July 1898   Many children are still away picking peas although notices have been served on their parents by the SAC.

There could be better days, and on one of them Edwin Capon recorded in triumph, 'ninety children present – best attendance'.

There were regular spells when children from outlying areas could not come to school because of the weather. Children living at Old Rowney were badly affected, having such a long journey to school from the far end of the parish, and no facilities to dry their clothes. But those with a long walk made some enjoyment of it. George Marston (born 1895) lived in Sweetbriar Lane and loved to tell how he rolled his hoop with a stick all the way along the lane through Mount Pleasant to school and back.

And what of those poor children of the 1890s crying because they were so cold? Numerous inspectors' reports record that the school was insufficiently heated.

31 December 1901: The main room appears to be insufficiently heated.
31 December 1902: The main room should be properly warmed.

In the large schoolroom, the open fire was insufficient for the height and space. The author remembers the chill of the schoolroom in the winters of the 1960s, when the daily milk ration had to be defrosted by the fire and the frequent tussles between children to get as close to the warmth as possible. But the winter playground made a wonderful ice rink, peppered with ice slides, and the vigorous exercise kept children warm.

Even into the 1980s, when the management committee was trying to get central heating installed, the problem was never really solved. The school finally closed in 1986, no longer viable due to dwindling numbers of children.

The gathering is the Old Warden Scout troop around 1912/13, with scoutmaster Billy Newton, also the estate clerk. Baden-Powell started the movement in 1907, and the village was quick to respond. Frank Shuttleworth, a keen supporter, provided the uniforms. The picture may have been taken near the Swiss Garden, a young monkey puzzle and rose arch visible in the background.

By 1915, there were many Guide and Brownie groups in Bedfordshire and the 1st Southill Girl Guides was registered in 1920, which welcomed girls from Old Warden. Both Lady Halsey, of Mount Pleasant, and her daughter, Ruth, were involved; Ruth being lieutenant in Southill Guides at the outset and, later, captain. Another Old Warden lady, Mrs Evelyn Diggle of Orchard Grange, was a Girl Guide leader in the 1950s and '60s, and rose to county commissioner for Bedfordshire Guides. Little is known of the history of the Brownies, but a pack operated from the school in the 1960s.

Scout Troop, *c.* 1912 (John Newton Collection, Manchester Archives).

Mrs Evelyn Diggle (Bedfordshire and Luton Archives).

6

Charity and Welfare

Visitors are requested to put alms in the poor box.
Written on every page of the church visitor books from 1845

We have been passing through a time of sickness and anxiety owing to an outbreak in our midst of typhoid fever. Some are of the opinion that it was imported by one of the painters from London ... others disposed to attribute it to an unsanitary condition of the village ... wells have been cleaned out, drainage inspected ... and water sent up for analysis.
Revd Lang, *Parish Magazine*, November 1898

Before the New Poor Law of 1834, each parish was responsible for levying a rate from its property owners to support its poor. Alms were administered by the parish overseers. Paupers either lived in their own homes or if destitute, in a workhouse provided by a local charity. The last incarnation of Old Warden's pre-1834 workhouse was built on charity land where it still stands; much altered, and still known as the workhouse.

A conveyance of 1650 describes a 'cottage and close' in Old Warden used for 'divers good causes', according to the terms of Edward Peake's will. Peake, of Southill, is remembered today in the name of a Biggleswade school, having founded a school here for eight poor boys in 1557. His bequest in Old Warden was for the poor and the repair of the road between Old Warden and Hill, 'which oftentimes with abundance of waters is very noysome and dangerous'. From the little that is known about Peake's charity, it seems that the early trustees (vicar and churchwardens) used the land as the site of the village poorhouse, and later added a school (*see map 2*).

A parliamentary report in 1777 noted that Old Warden's workhouse accommodated twenty people; Northill had room for thirty people and Southill, thirty-five. There are a few tiny glimpses of the early inmates. The parish register records a baptism in 1788 of 'John, illegitimate son of Mary Cresty, workhouse'. In 1813, William Smith, resident in the workhouse, complained to Samuel Whitbread about Bunting hitting him with a bell rope in the church.

A villager's despairing humour and frustration is apparent from the article in the *Huntingdon, Bedford & Peterborough Gazette*, 6 October 1927.

In 1828, the precious *Overseers' Book of the Rates and Disbursements of the Parish* was stolen from Sweetbriar farmer and parish overseer, Richard Garrett the younger, along with his folio Bible, Foxe's *Book of Martyrs* and a horse pistol. One wonders at the value of the account book to the thief – was there some underlying mischief afoot?

The workhouse, *c.* 1894.

NEW MODE OF DIVORCE.—The magistrates in this county have decided, that a married man, without a family, shall receive only the same parochial allowance as a single man. On Saturday last a man attended the vestry meeting of the parish of Old Warden to claim relief, when he was told that the magistrates had decided that he was to be considered as a single man; to which he replied, "very well; you say I am a single man—I'll turn her up then—I'll have no more to do with her." One of the parishioners remarked that he did not know there was such an easy method of divorce.

'New Mode of Divorce' (Find My Past). In the 1920s, the Scout headquarters was in one room at No. 29 The Village (part of the current No. 28). The Scouts had a campsite in Sweetbriar Lane, just along from Mount Pleasant Farm Cottages, which was used well into the 1960s.

In the 1830s, the workhouse was insured for £250 at a cost of 3s 9d covering the brick built and tiled house and outbuildings 'in the occupation of the poor of the parish'. It stipulated that 'no cotton wool, hemp, flax to be worked, nor oakum picked on the premises'. Such items were fire hazards, oakum being tarred rope used in ships, the unpicking being a common occupation for prisoners and workhouse inmates.

After 1834, new Poor Law Unions were established and the poor of Old Warden had to seek relief at the new Union Workhouse in London Road, Biggleswade (now demolished). The Biggleswade Union initially served twenty-five surrounding parishes. These massive institutions were designed as a deterrent, and became objects of horror and shame in the Victorian period. A few Old Warden people found their way there, particularly the elderly and unmarried mothers.

The account book of the Feoffees of the Old Warden Charity Estate (1852–1902) reveals that the former workhouse continued to benefit the poor from its rental income (*below*). In 1853 for example, there were eight occupant families or individuals paying rents from £2 2s to a minimum of 10s per half year. After insurance and maintenance costs were paid, the income was given out twice a year, as the following extract shows.

The workhouse, the old schoolhouse and the charity land (1 acre and 7 poles) was purchased by Joseph Shuttleworth in 1876 for £700. This sum was invested by the trustees of the charity and the needy continued to benefit. Entries for Christmas 1900 show charity payments distributed under three categories: eight widows given £1 each; eleven old men and single women given £1 each, and five persons with large families given 10s each.

In 1945, the Charity Commission listed four charities in Old Warden with the funds in each:

Lord Bolingbroke's Charity	£159	11s	6d
The Warden Charity Estate and Edward Peake's Charity	£814	14s	7d

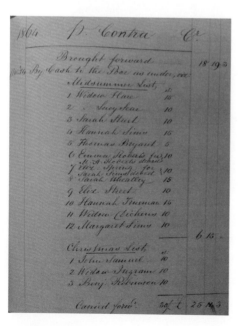

Extract from Feoffees Account Book, 1864
(Bedfordshire and Luton Archives).

| Frances Smyth's Old Warden Charity | £107 | 7s | 7d |
| The Shuttleworth Charity | £2,734 | 19s | 11d |

Bolingbroke once owned land in the parish, selling to Samuel Ongley in the late seventeenth century, and Peake's Charity endowed the workhouse and surrounding land. Frances Smyth was the spinster daughter of Revd Laurence Smyth, and sister of Revd John Smyth, both vicars of Southill and Old Warden. On her death in Bath in 1842, she left £200 to be invested in funds, the interest from which was to be given annually to the poor of the two parishes. In 1913, Frank Shuttleworth left £2,000 to be invested for the 'deserving poor' of the parish.

In the Victorian period, the village community operated popular Friendly Societies and Savings Clubs. The Female Friendly Society (or Sick Club) supported members when sick, in pregnancy and in childbirth, and on death provided funeral allowances. Women made monthly contributions, bolstered by annual subscriptions from the squire, vicar, doctor and wealthier residents.

Around 1880, Revd Potts of Northill was drawing up plans to fund a nurse for the sick and poor of the parishes of Northill and Old Warden, with Mr Harvey offering a house at Ickwell for the nurse to live in. Clearly the plans were implemented, as a nurse fund was still operating in 1919 receiving money from donors and grateful patients. The fund paid nurse Patterson for her services, insurance for her bicycle, and had an account with Boots the chemist.

Other practical help was available for the elderly and infirm. In 1898, the vicar announced that a wicker bath chair had been presented to the parish and would be kept at the Vicarage for use by anyone in need.

A Coal Club helped villagers make regular savings towards fuel (15s a ton in 1901), and, in a similar vein, the Sunday School Clothing Club and the Blanket Club helped budget for other essential items. Some charity money found its way to the clubs in the form of a bonus; the Smyth Charity contributing to the Sunday School Clothing Club, and the Bolingbroke to the Blanket Club.

Mental health problems were barely understood at the time. A favourite exclamation of the author's mother when her children were being particularly naughty was 'I'll end up in Arlesey!', a reference to Fairfield Psychiatric Hospital – formerly the Three Counties Lunatic Asylum – which from 1860 served Bedfordshire, Hertfordshire and Huntingdonshire. This saying is thought to have been common in the area, with many families losing loved ones to the care of the asylum.

Sarah Furr, a groom's wife of Old Rowney, was committed to the asylum in 1896 by the order of Samuel Whitbread. She was fifty-five and suffering from 'melancholia', the trigger being a petty theft. She had taken a few items of food from her husband's employer, and although he'd forgiven her, Sarah was pitched into despair over what she had done.

She had a 'listless attitude, repeating over and over again that she ought to have given herself up to the police and been punished ... sits all day bemoaning the fact'. She rallied slightly after she was admitted, but soon deteriorated, being described in June 1900 as 'miserable, lies on a table and will not employ herself' and, two months later, was 'demented, unimproved and eats rubbish'. Sarah died from cancer in November 1900, her only treatment for the pain being liquid morphine and liquid bismuth (a metal used to treat stomach problems). The carefully worded epitaph on her gravestone in Old Warden simply says 'Her end was Peace'.

In 1871, an inspector's report on scarlet fever, measles and typhoid in the Biggleswade and Potton areas provides a stark illustration of how Old Warden fared in combating the spread of disease:

> Clifton: Filthy pigsties, shallow wells near plait school, thirty to forty children in small room (mistresses' child in room ill with scarlet fever in corner).
> Southill: Clean.
> Old Warden: Model village.
> Arlesey: Filthy pig sties etc., fifty-one children in plait school 10 feet by 10 feet by 7 feet.
> All other villages filthy and overcrowded.

It is no coincidence that Southill and Old Warden were estate villages, their squires trying to ensure the best hygiene, cleanliness and order in their cottage facilities, although as the census makes abundantly clear, cottages were considerably overcrowded by today's standards. In the 1891 census, there are instances of families of ten living in four rooms, and families of five in two rooms. Even in 1911, there was a family of nine in four rooms.

The school was occasionally closed to prevent the spread of disease. In 1896, there was an epidemic of mumps and the vicar ordered the school to be closed for several weeks. Worse followed in 1898 when a 'general sickness' among the schoolchildren started on 30 September. By 7 October, typhoid was confirmed. The logbook records:

> 7 October: Annie Vintiner seriously ill, her mother has died of typhoid and her father removed to the infirmary. Edward Brittain ordered to the infirmary.
> 13 October: Geo Fisher (publican Hare & Hounds) down with typhoid.
> 14 October: School closed on medical advice.
> 6 November: Ethel Radford died, aged twelve.
> 20 November: Algernon Samuels died, aged seven.

The school was closed for six weeks. One child, Albert Gurnhill, was absent for four months, and popular publican George Fisher died, aged fifty-three.

In January 1906, no children attended Sunday school or church for two weeks due to an outbreak of measles. In 1929, a case of diphtheria occurred at Wood Farm. Biggleswade Rural District Council (BRDC) asked Tom Munckton, the estate agent, to replace the old kitchen sink with a proper glazed earthenware one. Tuberculosis also struck some of the population, and in the 1940s, Nellie Clayton is remembered living in an isolation hut in the garden of No. 28, The Village.

Four wells served the main village, the rustic thatch at Church End; a picturesque Shuttleworth version at Parsonage Piece; the workhouse well, where only the brick enclosure now remains, and Jacob's well, a grand statement of a well and object of

Jacob's well, *c.* 1898.

fascination for generations of children. Farms and outlying dwellings also had their own boreholes, but the village wells were low in the valley, close to houses, and there was danger in their depths.

BRDC had its water supply and refuse disposal arrangements inspected in 1899, with Old Warden incurring special mention. As to the outbreak of enteric fever (typhoid) at Old Warden, which cast suspicion on one well in particular, Dr Mivart says,

> Major Shuttleworth ... has decided to obtain an entirely new supply of drinking water for the inhabitants, and to lay on this water by pipes to the various dwellings. Mr Munckton, the agent ... informs me that the boring of a fresh well in the green sand some little distance from the village has already begun.

Local knowledge suggests that this new water source never came to fruition. In 1902, the parish council inspected Biggleswade and Bedford Water Schemes, suggesting preparation for the provision of piped water to standpipes in the main village. In 1935, the estate was asked by the tenant at Wood Farm to lay on piped water as his bucket of water had to last three days and his five-year-old son kept getting ill.

Although the parish council had agreed in 1945 that the village should be included in a sewerage scheme, mains sewerage did not arrive until the late 1970s. Householders relied on soakaways, cesspits or just emptying water into a hole in the garden.

Modern utilities came early to the Mansion House, which already had its own sewerage and treatment facility. In 1894, Frank Shuttleworth was reported as having installed 'the electric light representing 400 lamps'. The parish council first discussed bringing electric lighting to the village in 1931, although most village centres of rural parishes around Biggleswade had an electricity supply in the mid-1920s. The vicar agreed to three electricity poles being put on Glebe Land in 1932. In 1933, a faculty was obtained for electric lighting in the church. Outlying areas of the village such as the Tunnel and Hill Lane did not get electricity until the 1950s; Claypit's Farm as late as 1955/56.

In 1949, the parish council attempted to get street lighting installed, but at a public meeting in 1950, only five parishioners voted for street lighting with eighteen against.

Regular refuse collections generally started in the 1920s, but it seems that Old Warden did not get around to discussion with BRDC until 1935. There were always issues with night soil collections (emptying the privy bucket), the outlying houses and farms regularly being missed out.

Unlike so many post-war villages, council housing was never considered necessary, though it was regularly reviewed by the parish council. There are tales of bricks being delivered at the plot of council land next to Laundry Farm which was designated for council housing, but then quickly removed on Mrs Shuttleworth's orders. The estate could provide sufficient housing from current stock and, to facilitate this, people were regularly moved to more suitably sized accommodation. Joe Rowe's favourite saying after a death was 'they'll be getting the b****y wheelbarrow out now', in which to move tenants' possessions.

Parishioners petitioned the parish council to get a bus service for the village in 1932; initially a service ran only on a Wednesday and Saturday with routes to Bedford and Biggleswade. There was soon clamour for a better service, keeping local councillors busy.

When Winnie Marston married in 1925, she moved into a newly built labourer's cottage at No. 2 Mount Pleasant Farm Cottages. There was a bathroom with a cold water tap claw-foot bath and a basin, both draining out to a soakaway. Bath water was heated by a wood and coal fire under a copper in the outhouse, and had to be carried across the yard into the house. A rain butt supplied soft water for washing hair. The earth closet privy was across the backyard away from the house, and potties were kept under beds for night use.

The copper was used for washing clothes, and a mangle was the standard equipment for wringing out before hanging on the line to dry. Winnie soon learnt from her experienced Old Warden mother-in-law that she must never ever hang washing out on a Sunday for fear of upsetting Mrs Shuttleworth. It should be said that such deference was quite usual and even into the 1940s, Sarah Parsons is remembered for always getting off her bicycle to curtsey when Dorothy passed by.

Ironing was done using flatirons heated on the sitting room range, and Winnie would spit on the iron to ensure it was hot enough.

In a shady part of the yard was a food safe, constructed by Winnie's husband, as a place to keep food cool and free from flies. The cast-iron range in the back sitting room was the only means of cooking, and had to be kept alight in the summer, which meant the room became unbearably hot.

Right: Winnie Marston, *c.* 1923.

Below: A surviving copper at the workhouse.

Electricity only arrived here in 1952, and the family lit their way to bed with candlesticks, an Aladdin oil lamp serving as the only light in the sitting room. The front room was rarely used unless guests came.

When Winnie was widowed in 1959, she moved to No. 24 The Village, which was then a small two-storey mid-terraced dwelling in the old workhouse. She had two bedrooms, a small half landing box-room upstairs and a sitting room with a 1940s tiled fireplace downstairs, where the range had been. A tiny understairs cupboard off this room served as her kitchen, with larder shelving either side, space for a two-ring 'Baby Belling' cooker, but no fridge. Worse than the relative modernity of Mount Pleasant, there was no running water in this house, no bathroom, sink or toilet, but at least there was electricity.

At the rear across a pebbled yard, were a row of 1880s outhouses to serve each of the four workhouse dwellings. Winnie had a separate coal shed, which was dark, dingy, cold and dirty. Next door was her washhouse with ceramic sink, cold running water, but no drainage – just a plughole for the water to drain into a bucket underneath that Winnie had to take uphill and empty into a soakaway near the privy path. In one corner of the washhouse was her Victorian copper for boiling water and washing clothes, used until her death in 1969. A mangle was in another corner. In this room she prepared vegetables, washed dishes, and washed herself.

Like most families, she had a tin bath hanging in the outhouse ready for a weekly dip – in front of the fire if lucky. The warmed water was often shared within families. In 1966, her daughter's house, Warden Lodge, was provided with a modern bathroom extension, and Winnie could take her baths there.

Her toilet, a solidly built wooden earth closet, was behind the outhouse to avoid smells and contamination to any water supply. It was an uphill trek for an elderly lady, especially in the winter, and a bit later, a chemical toilet was installed for her … in the coal hole. At night she used the china potty under her bed, the next morning emptying it in the privy.

In the 1960s, the 'dirt men' as they were called in the village, came at night in a truck to empty the contents of each privy. The slow thudding of their heavy boots would be heard trudging round to each house, a slower gait as they returned to their 'night cart' to empty the heavy, sloshing buckets. For the author at least, the sound of these men of the night, never seen, always heard, had nightmarish qualities.

7

Gardens

Lord Ongley, has lately cheered the homes and persons of the poor of the village of Old Warden … and the gardens of the cottagers laid out in a style of neatness which, together with the natural advantages of the scenery, renders it one of the prettiest villages in the county.

Huntingdon, Bedford & Peterborough Gazette, 27 February 1830

I walked down the street, which was kept in the cleanest order; with banks of flowers and evergreens on each side. The cottages each had its trim flower garden in front.

Leicestershire Mercury, 9 September 1848

We went to Warden which is a show place belonging to Lord Ongley … there we saw the most extraordinary garden in the world, made out of a bog, full of little old summer houses on little round hills, china vases, statues, busts, coloured lamps – in short, quite a fairy land, but more of a Chinese fairy land than a European one.

Cecilia Ridley, diarist, 1839

Old Warden lies within the market gardening area of East Bedfordshire, centred on Sandy and Biggleswade, and is blessed with the fertile light soils of the Greensand Ridge and Ivel Valley. The market gardening trade started to develop in the sixteenth century, and was fuelled in subsequent centuries by the growing needs of London just 50 miles away.

In his will of 1673, Walter Caton of Old Warden left his two sons carrot seed, cabbage plants and a peck of peas. Parish records provide few occupation details, but gardeners do crop up, such as Walter Katin in 1697, possibly Caton's son, and William Bradshaw in 1722. The Vicar's tithe accounts from 1769 show regular payments of 12s a quarter to William Bradshaw. Other gardeners appearing are James Hide (1724), Richard Mathews (1749), and George Rea (1813), but whether they were domestic or market gardeners is not known.

The Glebe Farm land stretched from Bedford Road across to the walled garden of the Vicarage House, and an 1867 plan records that 86 acres was arable, 19 acres of grassland and 17 acres was allotments. Some of the sixty-four allotment strips marked on the plan have names against them, such as Bryant, Fisher, Willsher, Wheatley, York and Ward – all villagers. Most of the cottages in the village have very large gardens, designed to enable the occupants to grow their own vegetables, keep poultry and maybe a pig, but many also rented allotments and would have, no doubt, sold surplus produce to local farmers heading for the London market.

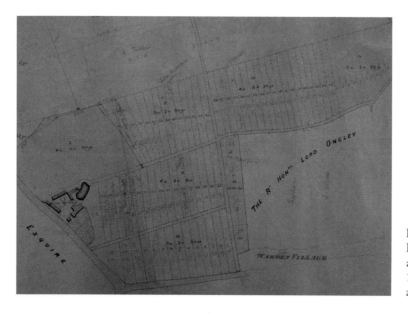

Part of the Glebe
Farm showing
allotment strips,
1867 (Bedfordshire
and Luton Archives).

Allotments were still held well into the twentieth century. In the early 1920s, William
Marston of No. 18 The Village (which has a small garden) tended the allotment strip
where the current Blenheim House now stands, as did 'Jocko' Brittain of the workhouse in
the 1950s. The cart paths that criss-crossed the fields of Glebe Farm for ease of access to
the allotments were used by villagers as recreational paths well into the 1980s, when they
sadly gave way to modern farming and were ploughed out.

Lord Ongley's Swiss Garden arrived in 1826–30. Mavis Batey in her article 'An
English View of Switzerland' (*Country Life*, 17 February 1977) wrote: 'The Swiss Garden
is a fascinating microcosm of the taste of the 1820s, combining Swiss enthusiasm with
ornamental gardening and picturesque architecture.'

There are few early descriptions of the garden, the earliest in a *Morning Post* article of
27 September 1832 describing an 'elegant party', possibly marking Ongley showing off
his new garden to the county gentry. Headed 'Grand Dejeune', the article says,

> The hospitality and attention of the noble host and hostess, and the elegance of the
> entertainment altogether were never surpassed in this part of the country. The gardens are
> splendidly arranged in imitation of Swiss scenery, Swiss cottages have been erected in the
> grounds, and the walks were ornamented with garlands of flowers; ottomans and sofas were
> arranged on each side at stated distances ... an English country dance (was) led off by the
> Marchioness of Tavistock and Lord Ongley.

Local legend abounds: Lord Ongley supposedly keeping a Swiss mistress in the Swiss
Cottage, their dead child buried in the garden, sightings of a 'grey lady' and mysterious
voices. Certainly servants lived in the gardens, as shown in Chapter 4. The most likely
initiators of these legends are the local people who maintained the garden, who may have
parodied a servant such as Hannah Palliser as Ongley's 'Swiss mistress'.

But mystery remains. A poem on an 1830s inscribed tablet was altered from the original version to describe a dead girl with dark brown hair and hazel eyes. The original poem, published by Barry Cornwall in 1819, is about a girl with golden hair and soft blue eyes. Is this a tantalising glimpse of someone who was close to Ongley and is remembered in the garden? Mrs Joyce Last, in her recollections of the garden in the 1930s, said 'one always gets the feeling that it was a shrine or monument'.

Another poem, 'The Forgotten One', was originally attributed to Ongley, and may also have given rise to the legends; it was actually written by Letitia Landon and published in 1835. She may have known Ongley, for an article in the *Bedfordshire Standard* in 1896 claims she visited the Gregory family in Biggleswade and the Swiss Garden, and says her poem was not written for Ongley, but for a Gregory son who drowned. Little of this can be substantiated, although the Gregorys did live in Biggleswade at this time and there is speculation that Landon came to Dr Gregory for the birth of an illegitimate baby.

The garden seems to have remained mostly hidden during the later Ongley period, although it was mentioned in the *Nottinghamshire Guardian's* gardening supplement in 1868, and had clearly been seen by the horticulturists who had written the article. Intriguingly, they said that the garden was built on the site of an old brick field and had been turned into 'one of the most charming pleasure gardens in the world'. It is not proven that the garden lies on the site of brick workings, but some underlying clay could have made this possible.

The earliest known head gardener working at the time Swiss Garden was created was James Beagarie (1770–1835), employed by Lady Ongley and later by her son, when he came of age.

Thomas Goddard (*c.* 1802–82) was Ongley's head gardener from the late 1840s until the sale of the estate in 1872. Previously gardener to a prominent Hampstead solicitor, he lived in Church Lane with his wife, Sophia. Ultimately, it seems that under Goddard's tenure, the Swiss Garden was not maintained as it was in Lord Ongley's heyday, as an 1880 article in the *Journal of Horticulture and Cottage Gardener* implies that prior to Shuttleworth's purchase in 1872, the garden had fallen into decline.

George Allis (1828–1907) was the next head gardener, already working for Shuttleworth at Hartsholme, and was brought to Old Warden after the purchase of the estate. He worked closely with Edward Milner (1819–84), the *Journal of Horticulture and Cottage Gardener* of July 1880 saying that Allis had 'the valuable guidance of Mr Milner, the well-known landscape gardener'. Allis had a good pedigree, probably working at Grendon Hall, Warwickshire, for the Chetwynd family, and certainly at Gunton Park, Norfolk, for the Harbord family. He was a Fellow of the Royal Horticultural Society, a fact he proudly declared in the 1891 census.

An article of August 1894 says,

The charming Swiss Gardens, Swiss cottage, vineries and greenhouses are now at their very best, and are a source of immense attraction – admission only being available by a written order from Mr G. R. Allis, head gardener ... who is always courteous with applications.

By now the Swiss Cottage in the village had become the head gardener's house with both Allis and his successor, Modral, living there.

William Cuthbert Modral (1869 –1946) was born in County Durham, his father was also a domestic gardener. Modral and his wife, Kate Whiteman, formerly the village infant

Swiss Cottage, probably showing Modral's planting scheme.

school teacher, both played an active role in village life. (Modral can be seen in the cricket team photograph in chapter 12). A 1904 newspaper comments that,

> Mr Modral has charge of all the paths and drives in the woods and grounds and these amount to many miles. A very considerable number of forest trees (40,000 to 50,000) are also annually planted by him, and he has just completed a handsome avenue of nearly 1 mile in length.

The *Parish Magazine* of October 1901 congratulated Modral on winning thirteen prizes for his flowers and fruit out of fourteen exhibits at the popular Sandy Flower Show. In 1910, it was reported that Modral must take credit for much of the success of Old Warden's cottage gardening competition as he 'takes an unwearying interest in the village gardens, and does everything in his power to encourage the men'.

In 1903, Frank Shuttleworth had established the annual competition, looking to inspire villagers to cultivate their gardens in a more profitable manner. Points were awarded for each vegetable crop grown with fruit and flowers included, and winners given cash prizes. The First World War and Frank's death ended the competition.

Mrs Joyce Last recalled Modral at Old Warden Park in the 1930s, saying,

> He used to bring a nice basket all lined with grape leaves, doing things properly when he used to take guests a basket of fruit from the kitchen garden. Every morning he used to bring the flowers and opposite to the housekeepers room ... they had a little room with a sink ... he used to do the flowers there. He had to put on felt slippers before he went round.

Swiss Garden.

During Modral's time, a Garden Wages' Book records a maximum of twenty-three gardeners in 1933, dropping to seventeen in 1938. The numbers included four women, and they were paid between 2s 6d (the women) and 6s 8d per day. In 1933, eight 'pond men' were also employed to dig out a pond, receiving 6s 1d per day. The gardeners' foreman was 'Wink' (Arthur) Shelton from Ickwell, his nickname reflecting an eye impairment. Wink earned extra money on presentation of rats' and moles' tails and destroying wasps nests, two-dozen tails earned 2s, and sixteen wasps' nests 9s 6d. This could be quite lucrative, as in October 1937 Wink destroyed eighty-nine wasp and four hornet nests.

Frank Copcutt took over as head gardener in 1938, and he later went on to the illustrious surroundings of Cliveden, working for Lady Astor.

Bob Bayliss, in his memoir *The Life Story of a Country Boy*, recalled being summoned by Richard Shuttleworth in 1938 to see a demonstration of a hedge-cutting machine. Bob wrote,

Richard decided to buy this machine and I was to use it ... One could push it along like a wheelbarrow and my job to start with was to cut all the hedges in the village and there were a lot. The tenants in the village were not allowed to cut their own hedges – this had been the practice for many years, and Richard with his mechanical mind had thought of a quicker way to do it. The whole village had to be done ... there were hedges dividing the properties and I had to do every garden in addition to the roadside but I did have a semi-retired gardener from the estate to clear up after me.

Bob also had to cut the hedges in the woods, set at intervals for the guns to stand behind in the game shoots.

A couple of quotes about Old Warden in the early twentieth century are interesting. The *Daily Mirror* ran an article in 1907 mentioning a visit to Old Warden by a group of delegates interested in housing reform, possibly prompted by Ebenezer Howard's Garden City movement. It said, 'Old Warden, a charming village in Bedfordshire, which although now almost forgotten, was the pioneer of "garden cities".

Praise indeed. Did Old Warden, conceived by the 3rd Lord Ongley in the early nineteenth century, and a caring succession of squires really have a little part to play in the thinking behind urban planning?

Arthur Mee, in his *King's England* series (1939), said in a similar vein, 'the last Lord Ongley set up his model cottages outside the gates of his park, one of the first bits of country planning'.

Old Warden parish council decided to enter the Best Kept Village competition in 1957, and won. The picture shows the presentation of a rose bowl. On the far left are Simon and Mrs Whitbread. The lady immediately behind the village sign is Ruth Halsey. Old Warden went on to regularly win or take top prizes for a medium or small village.

Best kept village presentation, 1957 (Bedfordshire and Luton Archives).

8

Crime

Warden is full of Vagabonds … I have found another clutch of poachers which I shall be at in a few days.

Lord Ongley, 2nd Baron, to Samuel Whitbread on 18 December 1811

No policeman is wanted, the inhabitants being apparently as model as the village itself.

Daily Mirror, 1907: delegates researching housing reform explored Old Warden's low rents and quality of housing

The issues that so exercised Lord Ongley involved poaching game, stealing turnips or wood, and even stealing from his mansion house. Poaching and abuse of the tough game laws was a widespread concern for the landed gentry. The penalties were extremely harsh with hanging, transportation or gaol sentences with hard labour.

Around 1723, Sir Samuel Ongley found it necessary to threaten his tenants with prosecution if they were caught taking his timber. He records in his commonplace book that, since coming to Warden he had increased his timber stock for 'the good of the Kingdom in Generall, and for my owne use in particular and that my Tenants should not want Wood for their fiering in their particular Familys'. He seems a patient and fair man, as he goes on to comment about the covenants made in his leases to tenants regarding his timber, and his many warnings to them, but he had 'not been able by faier means to cuer this notorious growing evells'. He therefore gave notice that 'for the future I doe barr and forbid all of them cutting, lopping, topping or shredding any sort of timber trees pollards or shrubs whatsoever on penalty of being prosecuted'.

Old Warden's miscreants appeared in the newspapers from time to time. In December 1774, the *Northampton Mercury* reported the escape from Bedford County Gaol of William Croote, alias Bignall, charged on suspicion of stealing a mare. Aged around twenty-four, he was 5 foot 8 inches tall, dark brown hair, a long visage, very thin and talked little. He was a labourer, late of Old Warden, and was wearing a light-brown great coat with white metal buttons, an old drill frock, buff-coloured waistcoat, leather breeches and a large round hat. Thomas Howard, the keeper of the gaol, offered three guineas as a reward for his return.

In the absence of a professional police force, various methods of crime prevention were conceived by local landowners who formed associations offering rewards for information leading to the conviction of offenders. Lord Ongley, 2nd Baron, was a member of the

St Neots Association for the Preservation of Game, Fish and Prosecuting Poachers, established in 1803. The Biggleswade Association for the Prosecution of Felons was also in operation from 1802. In 1829, Old Warden farmers Prime Coleman, Richard Garratt Jnr, George Neale and Charles Plyer were all members. Stealing horses, cattle or sheep attracted a reward of 5 guineas, theft of pigs or poultry 2 guineas, and murder of any member of the association, their families or servants, 10 guineas. A 7 guinea reward was offered for information when someone broke into Lord Ongley's fruit and seed house on 25 August 1829, stealing a drab-coloured great coat and a gun.

Parish constables were appointed annually to apprehend wrongdoers and take them to the local justice. Those elected by their parish vestry were expected to do their own jobs as well as carry out their duties as constables. The job itself was unpaid, but expenses could be claimed for tasks such as escort duties. Those apprehended were either kept in the constable's own house, the village stocks or the lock-up in larger parishes, before being brought before the Justice of the Peace. Old Warden had its stocks, and it's possible that a sixteenth-century barn at Abbey Farm was used as a lock-up. Local people still call it 'the gaol', and one of the constables lived at neighbouring Manor Farm.

In 1840, a new county police force was set up, headed by Captain Boultbee who was in charge of forty constables. Old Wardens' vestry minute book reveals that the parish was still nominating constables each year, until 1872. In 1857 for example, they were: John Hart the blacksmith, David Dickens the builder, William Whitteridge, the farmer's son of Manor Farm, and Charles Heading, the farmer of Upper Hill Farm (Hill House).

The outlying hamlets of Warden Street and Hill (then more highly populated) were served by a constable each, with two constables for the village. In 1872, Hart, Dickens, Heading and Harry Woodward of Park Farm were the last constables.

Between 1810–14, Lord Ongley's neighbour and local magistrate, Samuel Whitbread (1764–1815) of Southill, kept personal notebooks recording the daily cases he heard in his justice room at Southill House. He had a reputation for honesty, kindness and wisdom and many went to him to settle minor disputes. There are some fascinating records of the everyday issues and misdemeanours of Old Warden folk.

July 1811: Abraham Woodward complained that a man in his service, John Sims, had absented himself from his job and stolen wood from him. The constable was ordered to make enquiries.

August 1811: Harry Fir complained that his father had turned him out of his house. The parish overseer and constable were ordered to bring Harry and 'old Fir' to see Whitbread, who ordered the overseer to employ Harry and his father to find him lodging. It appears that 'old Fir' may have thrown his son out for laziness and draining parental resources.

November 1811: Thomas Collip of Warden complained that George Inskip had not paid his wages for threshing. John Furr of Warden also complained that Abraham Woodward had not paid his wages. The next day both Inskip and Woodward were summoned before Whitbread and ordered to pay the complainants' wages, and Inskip at least immediately paid up.

George Wheatley was caught by a gamekeeper setting hare snares in Old Warden. Whitbread heard the initial complaints and referred the matter to court. Wheatley was sent to gaol, but was released in June 1813, with consent of his prosecutor, on condition that he sign a deposition as a caution to all hare snarers outlining what would happen to them. He agreed: 'now I do hereby promise never to offend again in like manner and hope this will prevent others from following such illegal practices as such lenity may not be shown in future'. Wheatley had spent around eighteen months in gaol for setting snares.

Thomas Vintner of Warden was taken before Whitbread for possessing a snare. Thomas Butcher, the gamekeeper, said that Vintner sold the snare to Ellis Ayres at the public house in Warden, and that Vintner offered to sell more snares. Vintner's excuse was that he picked up the snare in a coppice going to work, the snare catching him by the foot as he went along the footpath. Whitbread had none of this unlikely story, and fined Vintner a penalty of £5.

December 1811: David Durden and Thomas Street of Warden were accused of setting eight or nine snares in the Swedish turnips in Seacots (Southill side of Bedford Road). Whitbread convicted Durden, and ordered a penalty of £5 but Durden could not pay so was committed to gaol for three months.

Lord Ongley wrote to Whitbread about a case of snaring in December 1813:

I am willing to give up the more severe mode of punishing these men by action. I however hope the justice will not show his lenity too much. George Saby is an arrant bad fellow, I am sorry to say; I have employed him for five years, and he has always been let the best jobs and earned a great deal of money; moreover I have taken care of him in sickness, besides other kindnesses. I am therefore the more indignant against him and I hope you will not spare him; he is a proper fellow to make an example of … I suppose the fellow is worth £200.

Ongley went on to say he was in favour of transporting a noted offender every now and then as poaching 'has got to an alarming height everywhere'.

Victims of crime, and those accused, had to make statements prior to their cases being heard at Quarter Sessions by the magistrate. James Beagarie was Lady Ongley's gardener. One Sunday night in 1816, Joseph Bunting, Robert Bunting and William Warner, all labourers from Old Warden, came at him in a 'tumultuous manner and made an affray', and abused Joseph Ireland who Beagarie had called to his assistance.

Ireland on oath said he was at Beagarie's house carrying out a task when a neighbour, Mrs Woodley, came and called him for help. He found Robert Bunting abusing Beagarie. Ireland told Bunting to be quiet, but Bunting then 'struck him about the face'. Some more men then arrived and 'made an affray', including Warner and Joseph Bunting. William Warner 'stripped and was riotous'.

By this time, Joseph Bates, the parish constable, had arrived. Bates found that Robert Bunting was 'in hold' but still riotous. Bates says that he put him in the stocks, however 'he with apertance slipped the lock and got out of the stocks. I took him again and kept him.'

Bates and Ireland made their marks on their statements, but Beagarie was literate and signed his name in full. Robert Bunting received a fourteen-day gaol sentence and a fine of 6s 8d. He was a young man of twenty-one at the time, and possibly his affray was encouraged by drink. He went on to be gaoled on four more separate occasions through to 1822, for snaring and violent assault. His behaviour in prison was described variously as orderly and well-behaved, indifferent or just orderly.

Joseph Bunting escaped gaol on this occasion, but the following year received three months for snaring.

William Warner also escaped gaol, but records show a string of earlier and later convictions for a William Warner; it seems this was a common name and there may have been another individual with similar law-breaking tendencies.

We do not know where the Old Warden stocks were situated, but they couldn't have been that secure, as in 1813 a prisoner is recorded to have broken the lock and escaped.

In 1834, Revd Neve completed a questionnaire for the Royal Commission on the reform of the Poor Laws, covering Southill and Old Warden. Neve had a single theory on the causes and consequences of the agricultural riots of 1830 and 1831 (the Swing Riots, a national protest by agricultural labourers against low wages and machinery replacing their jobs). He pointed out that there was just one riot in nearby Stotfold, which had no gentleman (squire) or clergyman presiding at the time. He believed it was this situation that 'such as would not improbably' led to great discontent among the population. In Southill and Old Warden, the leadership and philanthropy of Whitbread and Ongley, and ministrations of a vicar, combined to keep their tenants content, at base level meaning employed and fed.

Bedfordshire gaol registers provide details of Old Warden's villagers committed to the County Gaol, Bedford Gaol and the House of Correction. The following details are extracted from the gaol database constructed by Bedfordshire and Luton Archives. Of the 163 cases recorded from 1803 to 1856, just seventeen involve women, their ages between seventeen and forty-five with repeat offences. Men's ages range from eleven to fifty-eight, and there are repeat offenders.

The most frequent offence was poaching, then came stealing and assault. Hard labour in gaol meant breaking stones, being put on the treadwheel, or turning the screw – a futile task producing nothing. Prisoners also picked oakum, the unravelling of old tarred rope. 'Misdemeanour in Service' was the offence of breaking an annual contract of service by leaving the job early.

Offences committed by women	Types of Sentences
Stealing turnips	21 days to 1 month hard labour
Breaking branches off trees	14 days
Bastardy	3 months hard labour
Misbehaviour in workhouse	21 days hard labour
Stealing peas	1 month hard labour
Want of sureties	3 months or find sureties
Assault	1 month or 20s
Idle and disorderly person	1 month hard labour
Stealing a cap	3 months hard labour
Offences committed by men	**Types of Sentences**
Misdemeanour in service	10 days to 1 month hard labour

Snaring /Game laws	3 months hard labour
Neglect of business	1 month hard labour
Assault /Violent assault	4 weeks hard labour plus fines, 1 case of imprisonment for 1 year plus fines and sureties
Bastardy	2 to 3 months plus fines up to 23s
Stealing turnips	14 days hard labour
Not performing a threshing job	1 month hard labour
Deserter from 30th Regiment	unknown
Obtaining goods under false pretences	unknown
Ill behaviour in poor house	14 days hard labour
Cutting down a fir tree	1 month hard labour
Stealing or destroying trees and wood	1 month hard labour and whipping
Refusing to find sureties	28 days hard labour
Stealing peas, beef, a watch, fowl, a horse	6 weeks hard labour
Stealing wheat, barley, straw, potatoes	1 month hard labour to 7 years transportation (for barley stealing)
Stealing a silver coin	5 days (boy aged eleven)
Stealing railway sleepers	unknown
Stealing from a house /House breaking	9 to 18 months hard labour, 10 years transportation, life transportation and death reprieved to life transportation
Uttering base coin	9 months hard labour
Felony and larceny	Between 1 month hard labour and 7 years transportation
Negligently setting fire to a farm	18 months hard labour
Rogue and vagabond	3 months hard labour
Leaving wife and family	1 month hard labour
Trespass	14 days hard labour
Attempting an unnatural crime	unknown

George Wells, aged nineteen, was committed in 1834 after he'd stolen from Lord Ongley's house, taking a box containing the savings of groom, William Proverbs, and other items such as silk handkerchiefs, cigar-cases, pins and a brooch. At the trial, Southill butcher Mr Snitch produced the missing £10 note with which Wells had paid for some meat. Thomas Smith, the Shefford constable, caught Wells watching a play in Shefford and found various items on him belonging to Proverbs. The game was well and truly over. Wells was found guilty at his trial, and sentenced to transportation for life.

The convict ship, the *Lady Nugent*, carried Wells and 286 other convicts to New South Wales. Departing in December 1834, it arrived at Port Jackson four months later. There were just two deaths on the voyage, and Wells arrived safely. His name later appears on a list in the *New South Wales Gazette* of June 1843 as a prisoner granted a ticket of leave to move outside of his district. On 1 June 1848, he was issued with a conditional pardon ...

the condition being he could never return to England again.

The attempted murder of John Stonebridge, Lord Ongley's gamekeeper, received much coverage in the press in 1836. Gamekeeping was a risky occupation, with many instances of attacks by poachers. In 1815, the 'old and faithful' Whitbread head gamekeeper, Charles Dines, had been brutally murdered by a gang of around seven poachers near Southill Lake, with one of his assistants left severely injured.

Stonebridge lived in Queen Anne's summerhouse, and was checking nearby Hassocks Wood with his assistant, Samuel Butcher, one night in January. Three men were seen in the wood with a gun. When Stonebridge tried to apprehend one of them, he was bludgeoned and knocked to the ground by two of the men, while the third prevented Butcher from helping. Stonebridge was beaten where he lay on the ground, and again when he recovered his senses and tried to stand. Butcher eventually helped Stonebridge to get home and a surgeon from Biggleswade attended. Luckily Stonebridge was not badly injured and, having taken to his bed for three days, later recovered.

The jury found all of the prisoners, Thomas Albone and William Wright of Southill and John Merryweather of Broom, guilty of intent to do grievous bodily harm, and the judge sentenced all three to death. However, shortly afterwards they were reprieved 'the earnest entreaties of the noble prosecutor Lord Ongley who used every means in his power to preserve the lives of these unfortunate victims of crime, have had great weight'. The sentence was reduced to transportation for life.

Selections of articles from the *Morning Herald* on 'The Punishment of Death' were published by the Society for the Diffusion of Information on the Subject of Capital Punishments on 17 March 1837, and included an interesting article on the Stonebridge case.

The Duke of Bedford, Mr Whitbread, Lord Ongley and other landed proprietors in this county, are great preservers of game; but the evils which the system produces upon the habits of the peasantry are painfully visible at every assizes. One has but to take up a criminal calendar to observe that the country is thickly sown with game preserves, and consequently much frequented by poachers. A severe application of the exterminating law never has, and never will, repress those grievances as long as the great temptation to the offence exists, and allures the unemployed peasant to predatory habits, by constantly presenting itself to him wherever he rambles or turns his eye.

There is but one circumstance connected with the trial of the three prisoners to which we will particularly call public attention, and that is, the principle on which the jury recommended the prisoners to mercy – we advise all law-makers and judges to keep it in view. 'They had it in their power', said the jury, 'to commit murder, and they did not' – yes they might, if they chose, have silenced the only witnesses of their offence for ever, as they had them completely at their mercy; and their lives are now to be sacrificed because they abstained from steeping their souls in the guilt of a deeper crime. Public morality will certainly not be benefited by such a sacrifice, and public policy forbids it.

An example of opportunistic pilfering took place at Cold Harbour Farm in 1845, which may have remained undetected had it not been for the keen observation of Richard Girton, servant of Frederick Ongley. He had suspected for some time that John Chambers of Southill, a thatcher, was in the habit of stealing from the Hon. George Ongley, who lived and farmed at Mount Pleasant.

Girton decided to watch Chambers closely from a window overlooking the farmyard, and noted that when he arrived, he had several empty sacks in his cart. On leaving, the sacks were full. Girton, on Ongley's orders, stopped Chambers' cart before he reached the Bedford road and ordered him back to the farm. Matthew Reynolds, the Ongley steward, untied the sacks. One contained chaff at the top and bottom, but in the middle was another sack containing oats and split beans of about a peck and a half. A second sack contained all chaff and a third all wheat. Chambers admitted taking the oats, beans and wheat, but maintained the chaff was rightly his. Statements were taken from William Marston, the Ongley farm bailiff and his son, John Marston. It was William Marston's responsibility to say who could have sacks of chaff, which it appears were given out freely to those who could make use of it. Chambers created confusion alleging that Marston had agreed he could take some chaff, although he admitted taking the other items unlawfully.

Character references as to Chambers' honesty and goodness were submitted to the Quarter Sessions, but he was found guilty and sentenced to one month hard labour. Had motives been examined, the need for Chambers to provide for his large family, eight sons by 1851, may have been the root cause of his crime.

From 1859 to 1876, Bedford Gaol kept a register of prisoners with their photographs, taken to help identify repeat offenders. One mugshot of an Old Warden prisoner can be found: thirty-two-year old Samuel Goddard, son of Lord Ongley's head gardener, Thomas Goddard.

Goddard's crime in 1866 was 'uttering counterfeit coin', strange when evidence stated he had recently returned from America and had a considerable sum of £318 deposited

Samuel Goddard (Bedfordshire and Luton Archives).

in the London & Westminster Bank. He tendered a florin for beer at a pub in Caldecote, which he replaced when told it was 'bad'. But after this, he went to another pub where he handed over a half crown which was also counterfeit, so a policeman chased after him and found him with a bag of counterfeit money. Goddard said he'd picked it up on the road and had no idea that it was bad – an unlikely defence.

Goddard may have been visiting his father in Old Warden on the day of the crime, as he was on his way back to Biggleswade station to return to London, where he worked as a waiter. After his sentence of twelve months hard labour was completed, Goddard returned to London, working as a cellarman with wife Louisa, a tailoress. By 1881, he was back in Old Warden working as a cobbler and living with his elderly parents in their cottage in Church Lane.

Captain James Holford DSO of Mount Pleasant drew unfavourable attention to the village 1910. He was formerly in Frank Shuttleworth's regiment, the 7th Hussars, had a distinguished military career and was from a wealthy family. However, he was charged at the Old Bailey with fraudulently obtaining £4,000 worth of diamond jewellery; buying the jewels on credit, he immediately pawned them to cover other debt. He was held in custody for two months and pleaded guilty to some of the charges. However, the recorder was lenient and citing both his military career and recent detention, considered he had been punished enough. Holford was discharged from court and, unsurprisingly, soon left the village with his family. So much for that assertion made in 1907 about the model behaviour of the villagers.

9

Religion

Thou pleasant village
Warden is thy name
Renowned for beauty
In the list of fame

Thou art an emblem
Of that happy land
Where peace and plenty
Travel hand in hand

Thy sacred temple
Lately in decay
Again is opened
On the sabbath day

And is become
As all rejoice to see
What every church
In England ought to be

Fragment of poem attributed to Robert Henley, 3rd Lord Ongley, 1845

This poem commemorates the completion of Ongley's beautification of St Leonard's church. The people of 1840s' Old Warden worked alongside their squire to restore and adorn their church with an exuberant mix of richly carved wood, imported by Ongley from the Low Countries and Italy. The transition from a plain and simple interior must have been staggering for them. Ongley's vision and taste attracted national comment, and village pride was reflected in the numbers of visitors who came from far afield to see their church.

A contemporary view of the 1840s' alterations came from John Martin, the librarian at Woburn Abbey. He wrote in 1846,

The solemn air, and the grateful impression which the mind of the spectator receives on his entrance form a striking contrast to the chilling effect produced by masses of whitewash, and the appearance of neglect and decay. The rich decorations, the costly specimens of carving and the delightful order which prevail throughout this elaborately ornamented building, render it one of the bright spots among the miserably neglected churches of the county.

Martin was not without criticism, and was sorry to see enclosed pews considering them of 'selfish appearance'. He also thought the well-trained choir could do without the accompaniment of the new organ, which obscured the west window, and he didn't like the position of the double-decker pulpit and reading desk (seen on the John Sunman Austin engraving, pictured opposite).

Ongley also attended to landscaping the churchyard, seen here through the eyes of a visitor in 1848, who wrote,

> The first object that attracted my notice was the village church situated on a rising ground. I found the sexton and walked with him into the churchyard. Near the entrance lay a stone bearing this inscription – O Lord, we beseech Thee to guide us with pure minds through this holy ground of rest and peace. The yard was crowded with graves, each covered with a green mound, evidently preserved with care. Over some graves evergreens were planted; others were decorated with flowers. I inquired whether this attention to the decency and beauty of the burial ground was to be ascribed to the taste of the villagers; but the sexton informed me that it was all the work of Lord Ongley, the owner of the village. I was delighted with all that I heard of the good taste and benevolence of this nobleman. It is not an uncommon thing for a friend to decorate the grave of a friend; but it is a fact too uncommon to find a nobleman planting weeping willows over the graves of poor villagers … I looked at the interior of the church which I found fitted up with excellent taste. Lord Ongley had paid considerable attention to the cultivation of vocal harmony among the people, and the singing of the Warden choir was celebrated in the neighbouring villages.

The inscribed stone still exists at the entrance gate to the churchyard, with another on the path to the chancel door: 'O God may thy mercy pardon what I have been, may thy truth reform what I am and may thy wisdom direct what I shall be'.

In 1849, an article was published in the *Spectator* under the heading 'Art Ministering to Religion':

> Here is a church of some age which has been repaired by Lord Ongley, he has brought carvings from abroad; the windows are of stained glass, principally of blue and red; a few pictures, copies probably of an *Ecce Homo* and of the *Madonna and Child*, after skilful hands, supply, not images for worship, but objects that attune the mind to the spirit of sacrifice. The simple but picturesque forms and arrangement of the older building suit the repairs and ornaments; Lord Ongley, we have been told, was himself the principal workman.
>
> The church is situate on a beautiful piece of rising ground, with abundant foliage about it; the graves are adorned with flowers. Exception may be taken, perhaps to some trivialities in the ornaments; but upon the whole the effect is beautiful … The dark carved wood, rich and deep in tone, gives a solemn air to the place; above, heavenward, the white walls rise to a fuller light; the stained glass tempers the brilliancy, and casts lovely tints on the dark brown wood.

Above left: The organ set in the tower arch (The Shuttleworth Trust).

Above right: Engraving of church interior, John Sunman Austin, 1854 (Bedfordshire and Luton Archives).

Ongley clearly played an active role with the works, leading to speculation that he may have been similarly involved during the creation of his Swiss Garden and model village.

Not all saw beauty in the church though, and tastes changed. Sir Nikolaus Pevsner, critic of England's buildings, reacted with shock at the church interior when he saw it in the 1960s. He wrote,

> It oppresses you from all sides; it is utterly disjointed, and can only here and there be read consecutively ... The total impression is as stuffy as are those houses which early Victorian squires have crowded similarly with the fruits of their travelling.

Pevsner, almost as an afterthought, paid the briefest of compliments to the village, commenting on the very pretty cottages at the approach to the church.

The church continued to be improved over the years, with the restoration of the chancel by Samuel Whitbread in the 1880s, and Shuttleworth's considerable contribution to repairs, endowing the church with a new organ, memorials, stained-glass windows, and the Richard Shuttleworth memorial porch. This last work in 1952 removed the lovely Gothic porch and replaced it with a red brick and timber design by Professor Sir Albert Richardson. The inscription above the old porch reads 'Blessed are they that hear the Word of God and keep it' (Luke 11:28).

In the early 1700s, the Bishop of Lincoln, William Wake, sent a series of questions to each vicar to check on his parishes. Reflecting the concerns of the Anglican Church, he

The old church porch (The Shuttleworth Trust).

particularly wanted to know about Nonconformist (dissenters') families. In 1706, vicar Thomas Miles reported that the parish contained around sixty families of which five were Nonconformist, thought to be of the Independent church popularised by John Bunyan, but they had no meeting house. There were no Papists (Catholics). He also reported that there were no monuments of note in the church, and no antiquities of note in the parish.

Three years later, the curate in charge was Edward Gibson, vicar of Haynes, who lived in the Parsonage House at Haynes. Old Warden had around 140 parishioners, of which around thirty were Nonconformists, 'followers of one Killingworth who has a meeting every Sunday at Southill'. This was Thomas Killingworth, who was the first pastor of the Southill meeting house, which later became the Strict Baptist chapel still in existence today. Killingworth, Gibson stated, preached at Old Warden about once a month – probably at an outdoor gathering place in the village. Gibson himself provided divine service once every Sunday at Old Warden, and Haynes performed twice, except in the winter months when he could not get back in enough time from Warden.

In 1712, much is the same with fifty families, of which ten were Nonconformists. Gibson performed communion three times a year, for around thirty people. A licensed Nonconformist meeting house appeared somewhere in the village by 1717, probably located in a village cottage or barn, with meetings held once a month. It did not thrive, and was gone by 1720.

A century later, Archbishop Bonney's visitations of 1820–40 refer mainly to material and practical issues concerning the church fittings and structure. In 1823, he ordered that the earth be moved from the walls of the church and chancel to prevent damp, a common feature of many ancient churches. Also that the walls needed to be pointed and buttresses repaired, the stonework on the windows and doors to be restored with 'parker's cement', the west window of the south aisle be restored with stone and the woodwork between the church and chancel be removed.

On the items within the church, he ordered that the old flagon be disposed of and a new plated flagon purchased, as well as a deep plate for the alms. He wanted a new cloth to adorn the communion table and the communion rails to be cleaned and oiled.

Later in 1839, he ordered the churchwardens to repair the flashing in the south aisle, then clean the walls and paint a light-drab stone colour. The tiling on the tower also needed repair work, and the bells were in a state and needed attention.

It's easy to suppose that villagers faithfully turned up at St Leonard's on a Sunday, encouraged by the example of their squire, but this was not necessarily the case. If villagers were disillusioned with the Church of England, there was plenty of opportunity for them to fulfil their spiritual needs by travelling to other villages to join a Baptist, Methodist or Independent meeting. The Strict Baptist chapel at Southill attracted people of Warden from its inception in 1693, and many Old Warden names are entered in the surviving 'Church Book'. Some did not take their religion too seriously though, and Ann Honour of Warden was excluded in 1741 for 'neglect and contempt of the church'.

Among the many trustees of the Southill chapel over the years are the following Old Warden people: William Beaumont of Hill, yeoman, 1714 (a grocer in 1737); Edward Breadsall, lath-render, 1737; John Whittamor, yeoman, 1765; Robert Morris of Hill, grazier, 1803; John Garner, carpenter, 1847; William Marstyn, yeoman, 1847; James Berridge, yeoman, 1847; William Bryant, labourer, 1887, and Joseph Scott, rural postman, 1887.

The memoirs of Jane Inskip, née Street (1834–1924), who was married to William Inskip, farmer of Shefford Hardwick, include a reference to Old Warden and a glimpse of the efforts in travel many made to attend their chapel of choice. Before her marriage, she lived in Cople, and attended the Baptist chapel at Cotton End. She recalled,

> As there was no other Nonconformist place for many miles, the farmers came from all the villages round. I remember some from Riseley, Cople, Willington, Cardington, Harrowden, Haynes, Wilstead and Warden. These people took their dinners with them, and ate it either in their family pew or in the vestry.

Matthew Hanscombe (vicar 1727–38) succeeded Revd Gibson. He wrote in the parish register in 1732, 'This year I built the Vicarage House'. This may have been on the site of either Parsonage Piece or Orchard Grange. There were continual problems with the state of repair to the vicarage. In 1774, the vicar, Laurence Smyth, noted in his tithe account book that 'the cellar wall of the vicarage house at Warden gave way which occasioned the following expense; to Dickins (mason) £2 5s 7d, 2,000 bricks £1 16s.'

The parishes of Southill and Old Warden were united under one vicar by a Deed of Union in 1797, which lasted through to 1867. The beautiful Vicarage House in Old Warden (now Orchard Grange) was built in 1800, and the vicars lived there until 1936. Vicarages reflected the high status of the vicar in the nineteenth century, enabling him to follow the life of country gentlemen. The Vicarage House reflects this, even being equipped with an ice house. Beech Cottage became the new vicarage in 1937 (now the Old Vicarage), the last vicar to live here was Archdeacon Brown, who left in 1979.

The vicar wielded considerable power over his parishioners, and was next in village hierarchy to the squire. Local government was operated within the parish via vestry

The Vicarage House, *c.* 1930.

meetings, where the vicar, squire, farmers and other village worthies administered the Poor Law, parish rates (tithes), appointed the parish constable, sat in judgment on wrongdoers as JPs and were responsible for local roads, schools and public health. The vicar also ran and administered local benevolent societies and clubs. The squire had ways to influence the religion of those in his service. An advert from the 1900s for a laundress includes, among the short statement of requirements, 'Church of England'.

Two vicars dominated Old Warden in the nineteenth century. Frederick Hervey Neve (vicar 1816–43) was educated at Merchant Taylors School and Merton College, Oxford. He obtained a Doctorate, MA and BA. He became an active JP for Bedfordshire, and wrote and published a sermon called 'St Paul, a Model of Ministerial Duty' which was preached at Bedford in 1819, at the visitation of the Archdeacon of Bedford.

Neve was a hunting parson but a poor shot. In 1839, he shot 'one of the best pointers that ever went into a field' valued at over £100. He was out in Eyeworth with Montague and George Ongley when the accident happened, and the hunting party were so upset (it was George Ongley's dog) that sport ceased for the day and the dog was taken back to Warden for treatment by George Witteridge, who was considered an excellent canine surgeon.

Married with six children and four servants, Neve was quite wealthy. His will of 1843 shows that he left a trust fund amounting to £6,300. Legacies from his general personal estate of between £1,325 and £2,000 went to each of his six children. He had shares in the Regents Canal Co. and the County Fire Office. He left all his books to be shared between his children, the sharing to be supervised by a 'kind aunt'. He refers often to his old and valued friends, including William Henry Whitbread, Samuel Whitbread, Lord Ongley and George Ongley, leaving them each one of his books as a memento. Unlike his relatively poor predecessor, the Revd John Smyth, Neve left no money for the poor of the parish or for any worthy causes.

Within a few months of his death, his executors held an auction of the remaining contents of the house, which revealed how he and his family had lived. The goods were sold by local auctioneer S. Conder over two days, including

Genteel household furniture, kitchen requisites, excellent dairy and brewing utensils, and eight sweet iron-bound ale cask ... phaeton, pony-chaise, carts, double and single brass-mounted harness, carriage-horse and pony; three handsome Alderney cows, eight swine, poultry, and numerous valuable effects.

John Gerrard Andrews Baker (vicar 1843–80) went to Eton and Trinity College, Cambridge and gained an MA and BA. He had five children, one of whom he named George Whitbread Baker after his patron.

The 1851 religious census tells us about his congregation on 30 March that year. With space for 500 sittings in the church, the general congregation that morning was 200, the afternoon 300, and there were eighty Sunday scholars from a village population of 627.

Revd Baker bred chickens, specialising in White Dorkings, and won prizes at various poultry shows around the country. In 1867, an advert in the *Journal of Horticulture & Cottage Garden* wrote, 'The Revd J. G. A. Baker's Coloured Dorkings' eggs now ready, at 13s a sitting. Basket 1s. Post office orders prepaid at Biggleswade – Address, Old Warden Vicarage, Biggleswade, Beds.'

There is a tale that when the Diggle family moved into the Vicarage House in 1937, in one of the attics they discovered a room inches deep in chicken droppings, perhaps a reminder of Revd Baker's hobby.

On 26 June 1870, each member of the church choir signed the church visitor book. They were George Fisher, Joseph Scott, William Ward, John Wheatley, John Burrage, George Ward, Josiah Wheatley, J. Cox, William Radford, Ellen Wheatley, M. A. Ward, M. Scott, Jane Scott, Sarah Radford, Emma Butcher, Ellen Street, Louisa Warren, Rose Marson, Charlotte Hull, S. A. Wheatley, Martha Butcher, and supernumeries who were M. A. Wheatley, Sarah Ward, Emma Street and Agnes Hull.

With twenty-one full members and four extras, they must have provided a stirring choral accompaniment when all present.

The Revd Robert Lang (vicar 1892–1903) introduced the *Parish Magazine* in 1897, in a format still familiar to us today, with births, marriages and deaths, church services, school news, announcements and reports of meetings, clubs, entertainments all interlaced with a certain amount of missionary zeal – Lang had been secretary of the Church Missionary Society after all.

That first bound volume of all monthly editions for 1897, together with those for 1898 and 1901, still exist, providing much information about life in late Victorian Old Warden. In the second month of issue, the magazine was taken by eighty-nine out of 104 occupied houses in the village, at a cost of three ha'pennies. Subscribers could opt to pay a bit more to have each volume properly bound at the end of the year, together with two other popular periodicals – *Home Words for Heart & Hearth*, which was published by Revd C. Bullock and was a penny periodical for reading and general interest and instruction, and *Awake*, which was published by the Christian Missionary Society at a ha'penny per month to enlighten readers about the non-Christian world.

A shortened church service was held every Friday evening at 7 p.m. followed by choir practice. Quite often special preachers would attend from nearby villages to add variety to the nature of the service, and a round-robin was probably in operation. Communion was generally twice a month, and there were two services on a Sunday: matins and evensong.

Harvest Festival was a big occasion. The four church services held on 8 September 1901 were 'hearty and well attended'. As well as Holy Communion at 8 a.m., there were services at 11 a.m., 3 p.m., and 6 p.m. One was a special flower service where children brought offerings of flowers which were placed at the doors of the church and the steps of the communion rails. Later, the flowers were sent by train to the Chelsea Infirmary and the Children's Hospital at Shadwell. An arch was erected in the chancel and hung with clematis, hops and bunches of grapes, and the pulpit and font decorated with the fruit of the Cape gooseberry, apparently considered quite novel at this time.

Various institutions benefited from collections such as the Bedford Infirmary, the Royal Agricultural Benevolent Institution, and fruit, vegetables and flowers were sent for the inmates of the Biggleswade workhouse.

A full description of the memorial services held for Queen Victoria when she died in 1901 is contained in the *Parish Magazine*, right down to the text of Vicar Lang's address to the congregation, the whole encircled by bold black borders around the article. Memorial services were held simultaneously across the country at 2.30 p.m. on Friday 2 February. There was a muffled peal of bells and the service began with the Dead March played on the organ by village schoolmaster, Mr Wall. The church was draped in purple cloth, and it was noted that nearly everyone in the village attended. There was also a special children's memorial service on the Sunday afternoon, and almost every child in the Day and Sunday school attended, some wearing token mourning.

The rules of the Old Warden Sunday school were published in the magazine to ensure all parents and children understood what was required of them:

1. All children of five years and over at liberty to enter the Sunday school providing they attend regularly unless prevented by sickness, temporary employment in field or other work, or absence from home. The doors of the school are locked at the hour of assembly and are not again opened.
2. Every child present on Sunday morning is expected to go on to service at church unless excused by the special permission of the superintendent; children who have left the day school walking up by themselves, the rest with the Superintendent.
3. Every child above the infant classes must bring to school Bible, prayer book and hymn book.
4. Every child is expected to learn and repeat correctly the Lesson set.
5. On entering church and again before leaving every child should kneel and offer the prayer which has been printed and supplied to be pasted into the fly leaf of the prayer book.
6. Any child breaking these rules is liable to be dismissed from the school.

Each month, the weekly scripture repetition lists were published in the magazine, with separate lists for children of the senior and junior classes to learn and recite. Their endeavours were well rewarded with treats and entertainments.

Separate men's and women's Bible classes were held every Monday afternoon at the vicarage for women over fifteen, and Sunday evenings in the schoolroom for men over sixteen. Vicar Lang regularly published beautifully phrased pleas for more to attend, especially younger people.

Monthly missionary prayer meetings were held in the schoolroom, and the opening of the missionary box collections warranted a half-yearly special event, with boxes being opened promptly at 7.45 p.m., followed by a short entertainment.

Contributions from villagers to home and foreign missions amounted to £68 12s 6d in the year 1900/01, with contributions in each household missionary box published for all to see, down to the last farthing. The list for 1901 is topped by the Vicarage House and kitchen with £4 9s 2d, followed by Mrs Waby, the Shuttleworth housekeeper with £2 3s 6d. Most households collected sums of under £1.

Cottage readings took place every week at two venues in order for villagers to meditate and study the word of God and prayer. Studies could cover such topics as the spirit of charity, Christian watchfulness and the role of the family. A short half-hour meeting took place at Mrs David Wheatley's house in the village, and another meeting at George Youren's (later John Samuel's) house for those living further outside of the village in Warden Street and the Tunnel. Wheatley was an elderly retired market gardener at this time, Youren a former platelayer on the railway.

There were eighty members of the Scripture Union, the secretary being the vicar's daughter, Miss Edith M. Lang. Subscription was 1d per annum.

Church expenses were a problem, and early in 1897, the churchwardens were owed money and there were insufficient funds to meet the expense for maintaining the church. Consideration had to be made as to how to improve finances and announcements appeared in the magazine. Offertories for the church expenses and poor funds were detailed monthly.

Mrs Lang, as the vicar's wife, organised working parties of parishioners who made clothes and other items for the Christian Missionary Society. The CMS Sale of Work was held annually in the schoolroom, such as this in December 1898:

There were two stalls of needlework and fancy articles held, the one by Mrs Lang, Miss K. Whiteman (schoolteacher) and Mrs Sherwood, and the other by Mrs Waby (Shuttleworth housekeeper) and Mrs Foster (wife of the Shuttleworth stud groom). There was also a stationery stall taken by Maud Milliner and Alice Newton (school assistant) and a Christmas tree and toy stall taken by Miss D. C. Lang (the future Mrs Shuttleworth), Louisa Scott and Beatrice Aireton, which found special favour with the children as scarcely a single article was left. The refreshment stall and tea table were presided over by Miss Lang and Miss Whiteman assisted by Alice Scott and Kate Ward.

In the early 1900s, the village possessed a talented organist and choirmaster, Mr Charles William Wilde Birch, who was also conductor of the Biggleswade Silver Prize Band. He was a professor of music and lived at Drove Road, Biggleswade.

We end with a charming tale. A very special dog kennel stood in the front garden of Church Lane cottages, its tiled roof clearly seen in old postcards (and in the photograph of Richard Shuttleworth's funeral in Chapter 2). It was built to house Mrs Shuttleworth's dogs when she attended church, a tiny part of village history to be remembered.

10

War and Defence

On Tuesday June 18th, the village turned out in force to welcome home one of soldier representatives from South Africa. Pte Joseph Wells, 2nd Battalion Bedford Regiment had volunteered for service with the mounted infantry and sailed for Cape Town in October 1899 ... He had experienced great hardships and privations, and once had his horse shot under him, though he escaped without a scratch himself.

Parish Magazine, 1901

Dad never spoke to us girls or to anyone really about his time in the war. We knew that he had a nervous breakdown after he returned home, that he was made to be a sniper, was gassed, never took his boots off for weeks on end and suffered trench foot. He saw off rats 'as big as your arm' and his brother was killed on the Somme and Dad still had to battle on to the end.

A daughter's memory of Pte George Marston of Old Warden, 7076 1ST Battalion Beds Regiment (1914–18)

Back in the eighteenth century, every parish was obliged to provide men for military service. They were not expected to fight abroad, but were part of a defence force mustered to guard weak points along the English coast against invaders. Parish constables collated names of eligible men for the ballot, and those drawn out were expected to serve three years unless they could pay for a substitute.

In February 1763, three Old Warden men were chosen: Thomas King, Samuel Sutton, and John Thompson. King paid for a substitute. Samuel Sutton (1716–91), a yeoman farmer, paid Joseph Millington to take his place, and only John Thompson enrolled.

The Napoleonic Wars of 1803–15 generated great fear of invasion from France. In 1803, Maj. John Harvey of Ickwell Bury set up a volunteer force, the Bedfordshire Dismounted Horse Artillery, so named as they never obtained any horses. Captain Lord Ongley was in charge of the Warden Troop, and Dorothy Shuttleworth suggests in her church history that the flags flanking the Royal Arms above the tower arch may have belonged to Ongley's Troop.

Eighteen village men joined Harvey's muster, but some were not suited. John Simbs and John Wright were turned out of the force in disgrace, but Richard Simbs prospered and went on to join the 7th Light Dragoons.

In 1807, more men were chosen for the militia at The Sun Inn, Biggleswade, facing a penalty of £10 if they failed to enrol. Unusually, their occupations are known, but not what happened to them. They were; William Mitchell (butler), James Langley (footman), George Hatton (labourer), John Winn (servant), John Jeeves (servant), George Daniel (servant) and William Brown (labourer).

On 2 May 1811, Edward Simms (1794–1854), a village labourer, enlisted in the 40th Regiment of Foot at Arundel, Sussex, serving as a private until 1833. His attestation papers at the National Archives tell us that he was,

> In the Peninsula during the Campaigns of 1812 and 1813, South of France 1814. - In America 3 months, - At Waterloo, France two years, - In New South Wales and Van Diemen's Land five years, - East India four years 3 months.

This man, born in the village, served at the Battle of Waterloo and lies buried somewhere within the churchyard.

The Peninsular War of 1807–14 was fought for control of the Iberian Peninsula during the Napoleonic Wars, with the Duke of Wellington at the head of the British forces. A feeling for what Simms was to experience was captured by James Dilley of Southill, also in the 40th Foot, when he wrote home to his parents in 1811: 'I hope to God that my brother will never think of going for a soldier for I cannot express the sufferings in the compass of a letter that we go in this distressed country.'

Simms was awarded five medal clasps for his service, which included the Battles of Vitoria and Nivelle in 1813. He was awarded the Waterloo medal, which, 'for their steadfastness, discipline and stubborn gallantry on this day the 30th and 40th regiments of Foot were permitted to encircle their badges with a wreath of laurel'.

Granted his discharge in 1839, he went home to Old Warden where he lived with wife, Margaret, and their two sons, John and James. Old Warden's own Waterloo soldier was only discovered because Simms was recorded as a Chelsea Pensioner in the 1851 census.

Leonard Payne (1878–98) was the son of gamekeeper, George Payne of Laundry Farm and served in the Sudan campaign of 1884–99. The circumstances of Leonard's short life and death appear in the *Parish Magazine* of 1898. Had Corporal Jones from *Dad's Army* been a real character, he and Leonard could have met, for the campaign leading to Leonard's death was the Battle of Omdurman, about which 'Jonesy' regularly regaled the platoon with excitable stories.

> We have heard with sincere regret of the death of enteric fever (typhoid) in the hospital at Gibraltar, of Leonard Payne, who after having with his regiment reached Khartoum in the victorious army under Sir Herbert Kitchener and passed safely through the long trying campaign, sickened on board ship on his way back from Alexandria to Gibraltar, and was left with six other comrades in the hospital there, while his regiment returned home. And on 15 October, the sad news of his death reached his parents. He died in the service of his Queen and country, and it is a comfort to know from the officer commanding his company that he had won the respect of officers and men alike, and had faithfully and efficiently done his duty.

Pte Joseph Wells returned home to Old Warden for a month's leave on 18 June 1901, after nearly two years fighting in the 2nd Boer War (1899–1902) in South Africa.

Around 200 villagers met him at Southill Station, transporting him by wagonette into the village headed by the Band of the 3rd Volunteer Battalion Bedford Regiment. Revd Lang met the party with a few words of welcome, then everyone proceeded to the church for a short thanksgiving service. Thanks was also given for the safe return of Arthur Hare a few months earlier, and prayers said for three other villagers still in South Africa.

Wells was suffering the effects of rheumatic fever after spending over three months in a Pretoria hospital. He served with the mounted infantry under Generals French, Hamilton and Clements. He brought home a tin of biscuits given to soldiers on active service, four of which equalled a full day's rations, and commented that they were very fattening: 'if only you could eat them in the first place, and plenty of water was needed to make them palatable'.

He was only allowed to go home with his parents after the celebrations had ended, the family then living at Southill Lodge ('Squirrels').

The inaugural meeting to reform the Beds Imperial Yeomanry, a county based Territorial Army, took place in August 1901, chaired by Earl Cowper of Wrest Park. Frank Shuttleworth had already agreed to take command with his friend, Lord Alwyne Compton as deputy.

They aimed to recruit between 420 and 596 men, and raise £1,500 by donation, the government funding expenses and providing horses. Shuttleworth pledged £500. Each man had to be prepared to attend a fourteen-day summer camp and participate in squad drills and musketry instruction – it was crucial they could both ride a horse and shoot a gun. The annual camps were major affairs in the county, with several held at Old Warden and Wrest Park.

The yeomanry was a success, formed into four companies based across the county, with the Biggleswade Squadron based at Shefford. In 1914, many yeomanry volunteers came

Yeomanry at Old Warden Park (The Shuttleworth Trust).

forward for active service, their years of drilling, practice and camps standing them in good stead for what was to come.

To mark his appointment as commanding officer, Frank was presented to Edward VII at a Royal Levee in 1902. He resigned in 1906, but retained the title of honorary colonel.

At the start of the First World War, Dorothy Shuttleworth established a Red Cross convalescent home at Old Warden Park. There was also practical financial support for estate families whose men were away fighting. Cople man, John Ernest Storton (1909–2003) left a record of his early memories. In 1914 he lived at Water End, Cople. His house, like some others in this village, was owned by the Shuttleworth Estate. He remembered that 'during the war Mr Shuttleworth, who owned the houses, let the families whose fathers were serving in the forces live rent free and when the time came for them to be demobbed the rent was only 1s a week.'

This concession probably applied across all estate properties, with families in Old Warden also benefiting.

The Old Warden school logbook makes references to the Ministry of Food's wartime Blackberry Scheme:

> 25 September 1917: Registers not marked this afternoon as children gathering blackberries.
> 26 September 1917: Registers not marked. Blackberries. 191 lb this afternoon.

As well as picking blackberries to make jam for the war effort, children of the village were released from school to help work the land starting from as early as September 1914, when one lad was at work in the fields due to the scarcity of labour. In July 1915, two boys were helping Arthur Cooper of Manor Farm due to five of his men having 'joined the colours'. In 1917, the Education Committee gave an eleven-year old girl from Warden Street permission to be absent to look after younger children when her mother was working on the land.

After the war, the name of each man who served was placed in Old Warden church on a roll of honour. Thirteen men of the sixty-two who enlisted were killed.

Those who died are also commemorated on the village war memorial, on a brass and wooden plaque in the church, and by an oak or maple tree in the churchyard. Each tree has a plaque recording the name, date and details of where each soldier died. One hundred years on, the trees are now large, and the plaques still commemorate the fallen.

The 1911 census provides some interesting information about the men who served. They were so young, some clearly not old enough to join up until part way through the war. There are fourteen instances of more than one member of a family serving (a total of thirty-eight men). Of the Hayward family, the father and a son died, and one son survived. The two sons of Charles Clark, proprietor of the Hare & Hounds, survived as did the two sons of Sweetbriar farmer, Walter Elliot.

Three Newton brothers survived, sons of long-serving gamekeeper, William Newton. Three Wheatley brothers, farm workers at Oak Farm and three York brothers, farm workers from Tunnel Cottages, came through.

The Marston family lived at Mount Pleasant, descended from a long line of village agricultural labourers. Three sons served and two died. The eldest, Harry, joined the

Above left: William Henry Marston.

Above right: James Herbert Marston.

Left: George Marston.

4th Battalion Bedfordshire Regiment, trained in Ampthill Park and became a Lance Corporal. He died aged twenty-nine, on 13 November 1916 in the mud and fog of Beaumont Hamel, France, during a risky late-winter offensive. Harry has no known grave as his body was never recovered. His name is inscribed on the Thiepval Memorial.

Bert Marston had a spirit of adventure, and before the war, was working as a railway porter at one of the great stations in North London. He went to Canada in 1913 to make a better life for himself as a farmer but, in 1916 signed up to join the Forestry Division of the Canadian Expeditionary Force, charged to supply pit props for the trenches of France. He served in England and France where in 1918 he was injured in a logging accident and later hospitalised with influenza. He never recovered his health, for after the war, according to family stories, he 'laid on his back' in a Winnipeg hospital for five years. His death in 1924 aged thirty-four is recorded as being due to his Army service.

George Marston survived. His mother, Mary Ann, said that when he left home she saw a light shining above him and she knew then that this son would return to her. In 1914, George joined the 1st Battalion Bedfordshire Regiment. The only family knowledge of his service heads this chapter. The photograph of a jaunty George is marked 'Italy', together with his regiment details, and must have been taken in 1918 when the regiment was posted there.

Three sons of William and Emma Bryant also went to war. William Bryant had been a kitchen gardener for the estate but, by 1901, had branched out and become an electrical engineer. The family, which produced eleven children, lived at Warren Lodge. In 1914, Alfred was twenty-six, Gordon twenty-three and Percy, just seventeen. Alfred, already a professional soldier, was killed at La Bassée, France in the early months of the war. His two brothers survived.

Herbert Henry Bryant was an apprentice gardener, the only son of George, an estate gardener, and Martha Bryant. In 1914, the family lived at No. 47 The Village. Herbert was killed in action at Arras on 22 June 1917.

Old Warden Churchyard houses just one First World War Commonwealth war grave, that of Pte Joseph Potts, 2nd/7th Battalion Cheshire Regiment. Joseph was born in Macclesfield in 1898, and his enlistment brought him to the training camp in Southill Park. Tragically, just before his battalion was due to go to France, he drowned in Southill Lake while swimming. With the prevailing conditions of war, it was decided to bury him at Old Warden.

In the Second World War, with Old Warden Park again housing convalescents, Dorothy Shuttleworth sponsored a Red Cross Hospital magazine, started as a souvenir for those who stayed. Patients were encouraged to include their own articles. Issue No. 3 of January 1944 carried articles on the Fleet Air Arm, Old Warden's history, approaches to rehabilitation and a piece by Admiral Sir Lionel Halsey about the superstitions of the Maoris. Local announcements included church services, cinema shows, and the ENSA concerts (Entertainments National Service Association). These were held in the reading room (now the village hall) on Thursdays every other week at 5 p.m., a small stage being placed in the front window alcove.

A Red Cross survey found that the Old Warden Park cellars would serve as an air raid shelter for 300 people, the thick walls and sturdy construction providing excellent

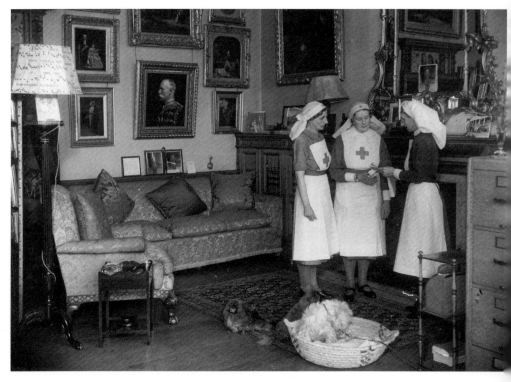

Red Cross Convalescent Home, Dorothy Shuttleworth and the Misses Willett.

protection. George Marston constructed his own air raid shelter in his back garden probably using knowledge gained during his First World War service. He dug a hole to fit his family of four, lined the walls with logs, covered the roof with wooden planks or metal sheeting and then covered this with turf. His daughter remembers that there were occasions when they went to sit in the shelter, but luckily not often.

In September 1939, an Air Raid Precautions unit was set up in the village, their uniforms not arriving until 1941. The ARP Warden's Post was at Laundry Farm with Alf Gale the senior warden and a team of seven village men and two women. The team won the East Beds area runners-up cup for their efficiency and keenness.

The reading room (village hall) was the first aid post with Mrs Shuttleworth, Mrs Diggle, Miss West and Miss Cooper nominated as first-aiders, although luckily never needed. A team of special constables, headed by Sergeant Modral (the head gardener), patrolled the village every evening checking the blackout preparations. Two constables caught youths stealing ammunition from the dumps. A proud moment came for the Specials who were on duty in 1944, when Queen Elizabeth visited Biggleswade to inspect the local battalion of the Home Guard. She passed through Old Warden to Southill where she stayed with her brother, Michael Bowes-Lyon, then living at Gastlings House in Southill Park.

The village had its own Home Guard unit: No. 8 Platoon. Forty men and two women served throughout the duration of the Second World War. Leonard Gilbert of Park Farm was Lieutenant, with Doug Foster of Laundry Farm second in command. Of the two

Old Warden Home Guard. Aubrey Pearce standing left, George Marston right, Len Vintner is behind the unidentified gunner.

women one, 'Glad' Noble was an evacuee. Ten of the men were veterans of the First World War, and others had seen service in the Territorial Army between the wars. A searchlight base was set up near Southill station, and another near Old Warden airfield.

The Agricultural Exemption Scheme enabled children to be released from school to work on the land. On 1 July 1941, Admiral Sir Lionel Halsey arranged for the school to be closed for a week for children to give assistance to local farmers. In the autumn, four boys, including evacuees, were absent in order to help Mr Cooper at Wood Farm with the potato harvest, and three boys went to help Doug Foster with threshing at Mount Pleasant.

Local bobby PC Sparrow talked to schoolchildren in 1942 about the 'Don't Touch' policy, as the Germans were dropping devices from the air to attract children that could kill or maim if touched. Children practiced an air raid dispersal drill once a fortnight by walking several times round the schoolyard wearing their gas masks.

The village hosted evacuees from London's East End and several other areas. The first arrived in September 1939 from Mitcham, Surrey, along with three teachers from Northwold Road School. Admiral Halsey ensured that the village and school were prepared and made arrangements for placement. Dorothy Shuttleworth was the billeting officer and for the first year of the war housed evacuees in dormitories at Old Warden Park.

School numbers rose to over 100 children, and the headmistress, Mrs Tompkinson, gained Dorothy's permission to use the WI hut for schooling. These evacuees returned home in December 1939, their short stay probably reflecting the confusion and uncertainty of the times. The BBC *People's War Project* holds a few recollections from evacuees who came to the village. In one, Norman Fosh spoke of his arrival in Old Warden:

Then started the worst seven weeks of my life. Somehow or other I finished up with about twelve others from another class, none of whom I knew and they were all very tough. We were billeted on the lady of the Manor, Lady Shuttleworth. Sounded fine but it wasn't. We were in dormitories and it could not have been more wrong for me – the first time away from home …I still shudder to think of the dinners in the village hall. Stewed rabbit twice a week; rice without milk which they cut with a knife and added some unsweetened prunes. The only good meal was sausages with delicious gravy. The village school was good and I soon became a member of the church choir … I fortunately caught mumps after seven weeks and had to come home.

Some evacuees had relatives in the village, as the school register lists parents or guardians in some cases as aunt, uncle or grandparent.

A larger wave of evacuees came in September 1940 at the start of the Blitz and during the Battle of Britain. Nineteen children from Dagenham were admitted to the school, as well as others from Stepney, West Ham, Chelsea, Stanmore and Cricklewood. Attempts were made to keep families together as much as possible. Four siblings from Dagenham were placed at Kings Hill: two with the Capons at Kings Hill Farm, and one child each to Mrs Gage and Mrs Shipp at Kings Hill Cottages. Eileen Braney of Dagenham went to Winnie Marston at Mount Pleasant Cottages, and her brother, Ronald, to Mrs Lenton next door. The children brought an epidemic of nits with them, to the horror of the locals.

The shock of displacement to these children must have been great. Winnie Marston's evacuee, Eileen, had never seen a Christmas pudding before, and when served up by Winnie, whom she called 'auntie', she thought that its colour meant it was burnt.

Three children were billeted with an Old Warden gamekeeper and his wife who had never had any children. Their clothes were taken away on arrival and they were given other clothes to wear. Again this extract is from the BBC *People's War Project*:

I remember going to school there and we looked up in the sky and the Battle of Britain was carrying on. The classroom was very funny because in the morning local children were taught in school, in the afternoon it was the evacuees. When we came home from school we had to go through a forest on the estate. Then they separated us as the lady couldn't cope with three children, my sister and I went to another farm … unfortunately we picked up other things. Mum and dad came down and we were literally covered in fleas … we had to be stripped down and ointment put on. When we came home Mum said we weren't being evacuated again. But unfortunately we were.

In 1941, another evacuee remembered a temporary stay with Mr and Mrs Clarke and her son in a neat little house with an apple tree in the rear garden. This must have been the home of Charles Clarke in Bedford Road. The child was delighted at seeing apples growing on a tree, and full of disbelief at finding apples abandoned in the grass under the tree. She later recalled in an article in the *Biggleswade Chronicle*: 'I remember Mrs Clarke watching us as we demolished a large plate of rock cakes which she had placed on the dining table. At home we had never experienced cakes being placed on the table for the taking.'

And what did the village think of the evacuees? The WI recorded that 201 evacuee children had arrived in the course of the war and that, 'the mothers and babies were from a very low quarter of London and the Old Warden people were pleased they on the whole soon returned, in fact the less said the better.'

Italian prisoners of war were housed at Highlands Farm, near Moxhill, and some were held at the Gastling's Army camp in Southill Park. One German prisoner, Arno Reinhardt, came to Old Warden as one of twenty workers transferred from Potton Manor to work on the Shuttleworth Estate. He worked at Home Farm and in Old Warden Park kitchen garden, slept in the Harness Room and ate in the kitchens. Like many other Italian and Germans, Arno stayed on to make a life in the UK after being discharged in 1949.

John Jenkins came to Old Warden with the Royal Army Ordnance Corps in 1941, later marrying a village girl and settling in the village. He remembers the RAOC taking over the Women's Institute hut, which had initially been used as an overflow classroom to help accommodate evacuees. The men used the larger room as sleeping quarters; the smaller room was their cookhouse. Another hut, later dismantled, was built nearby for the officers' accommodation and cookhouse.

The woods around Old Warden and Southill were used extensively as munitions dumps and camps. Ammunition, including barrels of phosphorus, was stored in the area around Lakeside Cottage, and there were three munitions huts at the Southill entrance to the Warren, which survived into the 1960s.

Palmers Wood was divided into five bays for storing munitions, with another depot in the woods surrounding the aerodrome. A rail line was installed between the church car park and Palmers Wood for ease of loading the ammunition, and around 7 miles of track was laid. Until recently, the tracks were still exposed in places on the footpath to Palmers Wood from the church. Lorries could only carry seven of the 9.2-inch gun shells and cartridges at a time, so there were long convoys backwards and forwards all the time. John Jenkins recalls that small arms ammunition was being transported to nearby RAF Tempsford airfield to be loaded into the 'secret' planes bound for France, and that shells were stored alongside Park Lane.

Avis Marston lived opposite Palmers Wood as a child, and remembers soldiers giving the two young Marston girls a ride on the railway bogies or trucks – war could be fun. Winnie Marston sold tea and made paste sandwiches for the soldiers who regularly passed her door at Mount Pleasant, and also gave accommodation to soldiers' wives when they came to visit their husbands.

The church, so close to Palmers Wood, narrowly avoided being hit by an incendiary which fell in the coke hole by the vestry during an 'all clear'. It was found the next day when the coke was still alight. In October 1940, during the Battle of Britain, two incendiary bombs fell in a field near the railway tunnel and the following month ten high-explosive (HE) bombs fell south of Lower Hill Farm. The Women's Institute recorded that fourteen HE and sixty incendiaries fell in the parish without causing damage.

The drone of Doodlebugs, Hitler's V-1 flying bombs, could be heard from the village in the later stages of the war. Avis, just ten at the time, remembers the eerie droning as they passed by in the distance, knowing that if and when the noise stopped, people were being killed and buildings destroyed. Sadly, tragedy from the air came to the village in another unexpected form.

A Mosquito Bomber crashed into Park Farm on 26 August 1944 killing the pilot, Squadron Leader Walter D. W. Bird, aged twenty-eight, and navigator, Sgt Francis William Hudson, aged twenty-one. The plane had taken off from Gransden Lodge airfield near

Sandy for a raid on Berlin the night before, and having delivered its 4,000lb bomb was almost home when it crashed onto the farm. The official reason for the crash was 'pilot error', believed to be the result of misreading the altimeter.

The people living in the large Tudor farmhouse were miraculously unscathed, including Kath Gilbert. She recalls that two Italian prisoners of war and two Bedford schoolboys were there helping on the farm, and four members of her family. Part of the Mosquito went through the house, including the propeller, entering through a bedroom window and out the other side. The room where Kath was sleeping was demolished; she was lucky to escape. The cow house and barn roofs were pulled off. The family never knew the official cause of the crash, but the Gilbert's nephew, who knew a bit about aircraft engines, noted that one of the engines was stone cold after the crash, and he thought it had returned home with some damage.

The Women's Land Army (WLA) had around twelve girls working on farms in the parish, more so during harvest time. Italian and German prisoners of war also worked on the farms, and workers came from Blunham Holiday Camp every summer from 1943, set up to give families from London a break from the bombing.

As soon as she was eighteen in 1944, Cynthia Linford, daughter of the Whitbread head gamekeeper, joined the WLA. Cynthia remembers her uniform being of very good quality: fawn-coloured shirts, dark-green pullover, corduroy trousers, knee-length wool socks and good boots. She was also issued with an overcoat, which saw her through two bitterly cold winters. Summer kit was a short sleeved white shirt with bib and brace overalls.

Cynthia Linford.

he was posted to Abbey Farm, then a mixed arable and stock farm, which was allocated ree WLA girls. This was convenient as Cynthia could still live at home (Gothic Cottage Southill Park) rather than a hostel, such as nearby Cople House, where two friends ved. Her wage was around £2 per week.

The men did the really heavy work. Horses were used for ploughing in the late winter /early ring, worked by the girls preparing the land for drilling.

Cynthia vividly remembers the exact moment she knew that the war had ended. She as working her horse, harrowing the field opposite Tunnel Cottages, when a car stopped the road. It was early afternoon and Cynthia was surprised as there were few cars out due to petrol rationing. She was even more surprised when a lady jumped out and n towards her, shouting, 'It's over, it's over'. This lady was so excited and was telling eryone she saw, but Cynthia never knew who the lady was. Soon after, the farmer lled the WLA girls back to the farm, and after tending the horses, they went home to lebrate.

The village lost some of its character during the war. It was well endowed with namental railings but the war effort required metal to be removed for melting down, tensibly to assist with making aircraft etc. Only the very best of the village railings were pt. Dorothy Shuttleworth's memoir of Swiss Garden makes reference to the loss; 'the vely regency screen (the gates) were exempted in the last war on the advice of Professor lbert) Richardson, as were the railings round the front of the vicarage and the school'.

The Swiss Garden Aviary was still in place just before the war, as local man Bob Bayliss members clearing greenery from it on the orders of Richard Shuttleworth. Maybe this storic structure was removed for the war effort – we do not know.

Old Warden's roll of honour for the Second World War lists ninety men and three omen who served. Five were killed, among them Old Warden's last squire. Arthur Jolly ed in 1940, son of gamekeeper, Harry Jolly. He was a driver in the Royal Army Service orps. Henry Parsons was in the Royal Navy and died with over 700 other seamen when MS *Gloucester* was bombed and sunk off Crete in 1941.

There are two Commonwealth war graves in Old Warden churchyard: Richard uttleworth's and Aircraftman 2nd Class Albert Ruth, RAF, who died in 1947. The Ruth mily came to the village as evacuees from West Ham in 1940 and were given an empty ouse in Warden Street. Albert was a talented artist, seen with his war scenes at the village hool (*next page*).

Old Warden's War Memorial, made from Cornish granite, had been officially unveiled nd dedicated by young Richard Shuttleworth on 31 July 1921, one of thousands that ere erected in villages and towns throughout the country. Admiral Halsey gave the ddress and Richard was assisted by head gardener Mr Modral. It is poignant to reflect nat Richard's own name was to be inscribed on the memorial in 1948, together with thers lost in the Second World War.

Albert Ruth and his war art displayed in Old Warden school, 1943 (Bedfordshire and Luton Archives).

War Memorial unveiling ceremony, 1921.

11

Visitors

Then thro Warden, a very beautifully placed sequestered dry village. So by Warden Abbey, where quitting the sand, rough clay roads begin. From the hill is a wild, unpleasant prospect over the Vale of Bedford.

John Byng 1794, *The Torrington Diaries*

A drive of less than an hour's duration through magnificent country of broad acres and woodland landscape, brought into view the lofty towers of Old Warden, from which the Union Jack fluttered in the summer breeze in token of welcome to the visitors.

Lincolnshire Echo, 4 June 1894, when 400 excursionists from the Lincoln Working Men's Conservative Club came via Biggleswade for their annual picnic

The diarist John Byng (1743–1813) travelled through Old Warden on his 'poney' many times during his Bedfordshire journeys, recording his colourful thoughts and observations along the way. Younger brother of George Byng, 4th Viscount Torrington of Southill Park, he particularly liked to visit churchyards and stay at good inns.

Byng admired the Ongley Mausoleum in 1791, comparing it favourably to Baron Yarborough's mausoleum at Great Limber, Lincolnshire, which he called a heavy clump. He considered the Old Warden example 'worth twenty of this, and did not cost a twentieth part of the money', a fine tribute for the Ongley's considering the Yarborough mausoleum was designed by renowned architect, James Wyatt.

Dismissive comment was made about the Hare & Hounds. Byng was happy with the excellent stabling on offer, but considered the public house 'not fit to be entered'. He left his horses at the stables when he went rabbit hunting in the local warrens with Frederick, his son, and their dogs.

Old Warden and the surrounding area can be seen through Byng's eyes as he describes the panorama from Old Rowney Farm, liking to visit 'the good folks there'. His description remains recognisable today, with the fir plantation of Keeper's Warren unchanged for over 200 years, although some landmarks are now hidden by trees.

To the right is a forestry fir plantation; keeping your eye, gradually to the left are seen the woods of Southill Garden, with the church peeping above the trees. In the fronting vale is the town of Biggleswade – every part of which with the church is clearly discover'd, when the sun shines upon it. More to the left is the grand forest, fir wooded hill of Warden Warren; in the valley is to be seen Northill Church; and, as you turn to the left, you view Warden church upon the hill, with many cottages of that village. More to the left, closing the prospect, you discover Warden Abbey, in grasing grounds, back'd by deep woods. I do not know a more diversified inland view, and only wanting the embellishment of some large piece of water.

Moving on from Byng's travels, there are a few accounts from early visitors to Ongley's Swiss Garden. In 1832, vicar's wife Catherine Young came to Bedford with her young son, who was studying at Bedford Grammar School. She visited the garden, describing what she saw as 'quite fairyland'.

In July 1835 Emily Shore (1819–39) of Potton recorded her visit to the garden in her journal:

> It is full of little hills and mounds, covered with trees, shrubs and flowers. Here and there are arbours shaded by ivy and clematis; in some places are little hollows surrounded by artificial rocks; in others are subterranean paths, besides railing, hedges, ponds, white tents, enclosures for birds, etc. Over the whole are scattered white statues and painted lamps, some on stands, others hanging from lofty arches which join the mounds. The principal object is the Swiss cottage ... which is surmounted by a 'gilded pill' on which stands a dove of white stone.

Emily liked the conservatory (grotto) best, which she described as being curtained in red and white and carpeted with coloured sheepskin, but overall she considered the garden 'in very bad taste, and much too artificial'.

After the 3rd Lord Ongley's refurbishment of St Leonard's church in the early 1840s, word travelled of its beauty and interest and people wanted to see it. Three leather-bound visitor books were purchased in September 1845, running through to the 1880s, and they have fortunately been preserved.

By July 1847, 1,000 visitors had signed the book, and in just over eight years (to the end of 1853) there were approximately 3,000 signatures, many stating 'and party' or 'and family'. Principal amongst the visitors were vicars, Northill's Revd Taddy and Wrest Park's Revd James Peck were among the first. The vicars from neighbouring parishes of Milton Ernest (Beatty-Pownall) and Bletsoe (Day) joined forces and came with their wives.

The local gentry and their house guests also came: Harriet Whitbread and William Henry Whitbread from Southill in 1845, Hon. H. Cowper, Lady Carteret and Lady Langford from Wrest, The Pyms from Hasells Hall at Sandy, Lord and Lady Enfield from Cople House, Lady John Thynne from Hawnes (Haynes) Park, Henry Astell from Ickwell House to name but a few. From Wrest Park came a titled party of Lord Frederick Leveson-Gower and three viscounts; Vansittart, Boyton and Frederick, accompanied by Revd T. P. Ferguson, vicar of Silsoe.

As well as visitors from Britain and Ireland, including one from the Isle of Man, there are entries from Paris, New York, Hamburg, Dresden, Mainz, Switzerland, Madeira and Jersey. A few entries can also be spotted from Old Warden villagers: Mrs Fanny Woodley and Mrs Sabey, John Neal of Sweetbriar and Mary Wells. An 1849 article in *The Living Age*, an American magazine publishing selections from the British and American general press, comments on Old Warden: 'the church is visited by travellers from far and near'.

An entry in the vestry minute book in 1868 gives indication of village pride in its church and arrangements for visitors. William King was appointed to clean the church on a salary of £4 per annum, together 'with the privilege of showing it'. Visitors probably received a guided tour.

Developments in transport brought increasing numbers of visitors to Old Warden curious to see Ongley's picturesque village and the newly restored church. Before the 1850s, visitors would arrive by foot, on horseback or by chaise. Main routes were being improved by the turnpike trusts and village roads and footpaths were managed by the parish surveyors of highways.

In 1850, Biggleswade opened its railway station as part of the Great Northern Rail Line, and from 1857, the Bedford to Hitchin line made it easier for visitors to reach Old Warden from Southill Station. From the late 1880s, bicycles gained mass appeal, and day excursions to pretty places such as Old Warden became increasingly popular.

By 1894, the *Luton Times & Advertiser* estimated that an average 700 people visited Old Warden every week during the summer, with numbers on the increase. As well as the attraction of the picturesque village and woodland walks there was the ivy-clad church with its carved wood interior, the mausoleum, the Swiss Gardens, Swiss Cottage and Old Warden Park vineries and greenhouses.

In the Shuttleworth era, the gardens were freely opened up to large groups of visitors. In 1899, 15,000 people were reported to have visited the garden and park for the annual Primrose League and Conservative Association Fête. The poor and infirm inmates of Biggleswade workhouse also had a chance to visit on annual afternoon excursions. The 1903 Imperial Yeomanry Camp in the park created comment in the press, when numbers

Visitors at the Hare & Hounds, 1898.

of visitors exceeded the expectations of railway officials and sports promoters. Crowds pushed through a fence, swarmed into the park and there was 'a general mix up of yeomen, horses, men, women, children, lances, bath buns, bottles of soda water and goods & chattels'. Amid all this activity, the report also comments on night-time disturbance to the camping soldiers – the number of nightingales which sang so beautifully.

Old Warden Park visitor books provide fascinating insight into the Shuttleworth's Victorian and Edwardian house parties, covering the years from 1884 unitl 1913, when Frank Shuttleworth was squire. The very first photograph shows around 200 Victorian visitors arranged in front of the Swiss Cottage attending a constitutional Fête in Swiss Garden. House party guests signed their names on a single page, often accompanied by a photograph of them arranged on the entrance steps to the house, and there are many photographs of shoots and game lists.

Who were among the Shuttleworth guests? A group of signatures for 1885 are identified as Frances, Dowager Duchess of Marlborough and her three daughters: Rosamonde with her husband William, 2nd Baron de Ramsey, Georgiana and her husband Richard Curzon, 4th Earl Howe, and Sarah Spencer-Churchill, who famously became the first ever female war correspondent when she was asked to cover the Second Boer War.

Later, in 1890, are the signatures of George Curzon, Lord Curzon of Kedleston and Mary Victoria Leiter, an American heiress. This couple married in 1895, and became Viceroy and Vicereine of India.

There are Harbords of Gunton Hall in Suffolk, the Earl of Scarborough, the Earl of Stradbroke of Henham Park, Suffolk and Baron Hindlip. The second son of the 4th Earl of Warwick, Alwyn Greville and his wife, Mabel and sister, Eva, were guests in 1892. The Hon. William Lowther, a diplomat, conservative MP and Bedfordshire JP visited together with his wife, Alice, and his two daughters. Alice Lowther was the daughter of Lord Wensleydale who was tenant of Ampthill Park House.

Locals were Sir Arthur Peel of Sandy Lodge, MP and Speaker of the House of Commons, together with his daughter Julia; the Thynnes of Haynes Park, Pym's of Sandy, Whitbread's of Southill, and Harvey of Ickwell, as well as members of the Lang family after their daughter's marriage to Frank Shuttleworth in 1902.

The family's Lincoln heritage is represented by many visits from Alfred Shuttleworth, and Nathaniel Clayton, Joseph Shuttleworth's business partner and brother in law.

Among the visitors to the village was Charlotte Bousfield of Bedford, who kept diaries about her life in the late Victorian period. On 21 May 1881, she wrote,

> This afternoon Papa has driven us to Warden, where we put the horse up and had tea in the only inn in the place. The weather … could not possibly have been more delightful for our ride which we all thoroughly enjoyed. John went before us on his bicycle.

Charlotte was fifty-three at the time, and 'Papa' was her husband, Edward.

Her entry on 31 July 1884 describes the different methods of transport used by her party of six to reach the arbour at the Hare & Hounds for tea.

OLD WARDEN, BIGGLESWADE.

Date 1904 Dec 7·8·9	Hilton Carte	The Warren &c	Irone Wood &c	Total
PHEASANTS	201	365	1220	1786
PARTRIDGES	14	81	4	99
HARES	17	71	1	89
RABBITS	1	5	10	16
WOODCOCK	3	2		5
SNIPE				
WILD DUCKS				
VARIOUS	5	3	4	12
TOTAL	241	527	1239	2007

Game List, 1904 (The Shuttleworth Trust).

The bag, Frank Shuttleworth standing on left (The Shuttleworth Trust).

A house party, Frank Shuttleworth lying in the foreground (The Shuttleworth Trust).

On Saturday, John came down early in the afternoon. I met him at the station with Aunt Jenny and Bessie, when he drove us to Warden where we were to meet Papa and Lottie who started before us with the tricycle expecting we should overtake them. As we did not do so John drove back, while I took Aunty and Bessie into the woods. On our return to the inn we found they had arrived, but the tricycle had hindered instead of helped their journey, the rubber band (tyre) having come off one wheel almost directly after starting, so that Papa was glad to send it back by a man, and then walking on to Cardington they were just in time for the train to Southill.

Tea in the arbour is one great attraction to Warden, but a nest of wasps having found it a pleasant spot also we were obliged to adjourn to a seat in the garden … too much wind and rain coming on, we sheltered in the arbour where the wasps seemed to rest. I very boldly led the way but paid for my temerity by bringing one away in my dress and getting a sting.

As there is no evening train from Southill, two of our party were obliged to walk homeward so I started with Papa again … When John overtook us driving, I took his place and drove some distance beyond Cardington when Jenny and Bessie walked and I returned for Papa and John who had reached the Green. Lottie was too foot-sore to walk again but we all reached home nearly at the same time not much the worse for our small adventures.

The *Luton Times & Advertiser* ran a regular column called 'Outings and Treats'. Many organisations and employers chose Old Warden as the venue for their annual outing and the Hare & Hounds tea gardens must have benefited enormously by providing teas and dinners.

In 1902, the Slip End church choir held their annual outing. Around seventy people came by brake, a motorised vehicle and, on arrival, had luncheon before taking a tour of the gardens and church by permission of Colonel Shuttleworth. Games in the woods took place after tea and the party left at 7.30 p.m., arriving back at Slip End by 11.30 p.m.

Forty people from Wellington Street choir in Luton came to Old Warden by brake in 1904, some following on bicycles. Stopping at Silsoe en route, they walked through Wrest Park, and at Warden they visited the church and 'scattered among the pines', followed by tea at the Hare & Hounds, then games and a return to Luton.

Ninety employees of Walsh & Son, Luton, came for their 1905 annual outing. Dinner and tea were served at the Hare & Hounds, and 'the chief event of the day was the cricket match, in which the single inflicted a severe defeat on the married'. Home was reached about midnight.

In 1908, the Barton Bellringers rang the bells of Old Warden church, followed by 'inspection of the beautiful grounds of Colonel Shuttleworth' and tea at, where else, the Hare & Hounds.

Motor tours were also popular, and Elizabeth Yardley wrote a diary of her drive through France and England in the autumn of 1911, her itinerary taking her through Old Warden:

We drove through a low-lying level drowsy land of deep green meadows freshened by little lazy streams to the orchard embowered village of Old Warden. This village which is full of quaint houses with carved barge boards, red painted doors and windows, was long the residence of the Lords Ongley who lived in Warden House.

Hare & Hounds tea gardens (Bedfordshire and Luton Archives).

She went on to Warden Abbey and heard about Warden Pears before driving to Elstow 'past acres of hops waving their tender green vines laden with blossoms ready for gathering.'

Yardley's observations reveal that the Ongley 'Swiss' colour scheme for the village was still in existence as late as 1911, and close inspection of Victorian and Edwardian postcards show the window frames of most cottages were a dark colour, matching the doors. By the 1920s the series of black-and-white postcards produced show that the windows were now white.

Postcards of photogenic Old Warden were extremely popular. In 1898, the *Luton Times & Advertiser* ran a promotion for A. J. Anderson & Co., the Luton-based stationer and postcard publisher.

> The little village of Old Warden, which is considered to be one of the prettiest in the South of England, has become popular as an ideal place in which to spend a day's holiday. During the summer Messrs Anderson & Co. have taken a number of excellent photographs of the village and church, and this week are making a special show in their window in Wellington Street of Old Warden and Silsoe views, which are artistically framed, making most acceptable presents, and should be seen by everyone.

There are well over 100 different postcard scenes of Old Warden, manufactured by different companies at various times. Villagers themselves sent postcards to friends or relatives with simple messages and greetings. When Clara Marston left Old Warden to go into service at a big house in Essex, her friends, Effie and Geoff Mayes from the post office at Parsonage Piece regularly sent her postcards of village scenes. People kept collections of popular postcards in albums as souvenirs of their trips, and sent them to friends using a ha'penny stamp.

The average number of visitors to the church in the 1950s was around 2,000 a year. With ease of international travel, people now came from all over the world, many from America, Europe, Scandinavia and even the Far East, Australia and Africa. The opening of the Agricultural College in 1946, and the Shuttleworth Collection in 1963, encouraged a wider range of visitors, not always with the best outcome for villagers. While college students caused upset by dangerously speeding through the village and country lanes, peaceful summer weekends could be marred by the amount of traffic passing through to see the air displays.

The *East Beds Courier* ran a front page article in July 1971 headed 'The Jambusters', with a photograph of cars nose to tail along Bedford Road and parked along the verges:

> East Bedfordshire Police battled for hours on Sunday to sort out one of the biggest traffic jams in the area for years, when thousands of people packed Old Warden for the Shuttleworth Collection's Military Air Pageant. By 11.30 a.m., a 3-mile queue was backing up onto the A1 at Biggleswade.

Caldecote and Southill were choked with cars parked on the verges and in the road, with people walking many miles to the event. The official car park was estimated to be packed with 5,000 cars.

But there were some advantages. Later in the '70s came a spine-tingling moment when the distinctive shape of Concorde flew low over the village, an airborne visitor to enthral crowds at the aerodrome and villagers alike.

A final thought for those summer visitors who no longer arrive. The nightingales which disturbed the sleep of the Yeomanry are alas no more. Nightjars used to churr from the bracken and clearings in the warren into the 1960s, but are no longer heard. Palmers Wood used to be so full of cuckoos that in the late 1930s, Joe Lenton, cursing and swearing at their incessant calling, nearly swallowed his lit cigarette and was unable to eat for days.

12

Fun, Games and Entertainment

About the middle of the village, I found an inclosed playground fitted up with swings and other instruments of pastime. Here the young Wardenites were gambolling with bats and balls supplied by Lord Ongley.

Joseph Gostwick, 1848, *Tales, Essays and Poems*

Ongley's playground is marked on the 1872 estate sale map, and was the site where the new village school was built in 1875. The little observation recorded by a visitor conjures up a bucolic image of leisure time in an early Victorian estate village, with a benevolent squire providing amusement for his tenants. We must not be deceived, however, as at this time children as young as eight or nine were still working long hours on the land.

Rural agricultural communities had to make their own amusements when and if time was available. If you were lucky, some entertainments were laid on by the squire or the vicar, and others could be reached after a small journey to other local towns or villages.

The ancient spring celebration of May Day has been famously perpetuated at nearby Ickwell, and Old Warden's people would have been attracted to the festivities and rituals well before it was decided, around 1912, to include schoolchildren from Old Warden in the dances around the Maypole. Warden Warren supplied a larch tree for the Maypole in 1872, and again in 1911. Every third year it was the turn of Old Warden to choose a May Queen, pages and maids of honour, but schoolchildren took part in the dancing every year, watched by their proud families. The author, herself a maid of honour and dancer on many occasions in the early 1960s, remembers the excitement of learning the various ribbon plaits, cat's cradle, spider's web and always last, the Circassian Circle. The younger girls, wearing flower-themed dresses, would skip up to a 'dame' holding a microphone and speak a little couplet such as, 'Two little Rosebuds, sweet are we. Just come our Queen of May to see'.

Another pleasure fair was the annual Shefford Feast, a street fair traditionally held on 11 October, and one of several ancient charter fairs in this small town. Villagers made the short trip to Shefford to enjoy the funfair, games and stalls. It wasn't just that a good time could be had, for fairs were a way for people in the area to meet, make friends, do business and even find wives and husbands. George Marston met his future wife here in the early 1920s, a girl from Meppershall. Children played truant from school to go to the fair. A logbook entry in October 1892 recorded several absentees gone to Shefford Fair, and later a mention of children going to a fair at Deadman's Cross.

Ickwell May Day, *c.* 1930.

Sir Samuel Ongley enjoyed feasts as well, but of another kind. He was clearly so impressed by Lord Torrington's dinner at Southill for 'the Gentlemen of the Clubb' in July 1723, that he recorded the menu in his *Commonplace Book*:

First Course	Second Course	Third Course
Soope	Chicking	Gellys
Fish	Pease	Sullybubs
Pasty	Artichoks	Churrys
Fillett of Veale	Pigons	Goosberys
Puding	Codling and Crreame Tart	Rasberys and Cream
Goose	Currants Redd and whit	

Religious festivals, such as Harvest and Christmas, were occasions for a short time away from daily toil. Tenant farmer Charles Capon held his 1901 Harvest Home celebration in one of the large barns at Hill Farm, where seventy workers and their families sat down to a meal together. The barn was decorated with Chinese lanterns and, during the evening, various toasts and songs were given by those attending. After the speeches, the national anthem was sung. In his speech, Farmer Capon said he 'considered that such social gatherings tended to bring the masters and men more together, which was a great advantage to all concerned in agriculture'.

A rare reference to an Ongley Christmas appears in an 1814 newspaper, when on New Year's Day Lord Ongley 'as usual' entertained his tenantry with their Christmas festival.

But the real fun for the squire was the meet of greyhounds at Cotton End attended by Ongley, Whitbread and other local gentry, all noted for their 'superior breed' of dogs.

Frank Shuttleworth gave a magical Christmas treat to village schoolchildren in January 1901, just one example of many over the years. It was, as with most events at this time, held at the school.

> The room was most tastefully decorated with ivy wreaths and flags and a beautiful Christmas tree on which the presents were hung, stood in one corner, the object of supreme interest throughout the evening. Tea was at 5, eighty-eight children of the Sunday and Day schools, with ten other guests, teachers, etc. sat down. After tea a selection of songs, recitations and readings was given by the children. At 7 o'clock the tree was lit up and the presents distributed. At 8 o'clock the evening closed with 'God Save the Queen'. Each young guest departed armed with present, an orange and a bun.

The Women's Institute carried on the tradition of children's Christmas parties into the 1960s and beyond, using their hut as the venue. Presents were hidden in the ever popular bran tub, games such as musical chairs were played and a tea was provided.

The only beerhouse was The Plough in Warden Street, known locally to have been at the site of the last cottage before Park Farm. Beer Houses were introduced by the 1830 Beerhouse Act, and anyone with two guineas to spare could apply for a licence and set up shop, often in their front room. They could buy in the beer from a local brewer or set up their own brew house. Beer was considered a healthy drink, was less likely than well water to be contaminated, and it was thought that by establishing premises selling just beer, the young labourer would be less inclined to turn to more disabling drinks such as gin.

The Barnett family ran The Plough from the 1840s to the early 1870s and it closed in 1877, when Jonah Elms was the proprietor. In its heyday it may have drawn in agricultural labourers from the surrounding farms, Abbey and Manor, Park and Wood, Sweetbriar and Mount Pleasant. With the building of the railway in the 1850s, came navvies and new housing at Tunnel Cottages. After a lonely day in the fields, the beerhouse would have been a place for young men to meet and catch up.

The mechanisation of agriculture and drift to the towns and industrial cities may have caused The Plough to lose trade, but equally, it can't have been a pleasant place in which to spend any time. Plans drawn up for Joseph Shuttleworth show the site consisted of a pantiled hovel 'in bad repair', a shed covered with felt, 'falling down', a pantiled barn, a lath and plaster two-up two-down house 'in very bad repair' adjoining which was the tap room in 'the very worst state of repair'. To cap it all, a pencil note on the plan says there was no well, just a small pond of impure water.

The village public house first appears in a deed of 1792, when it was called The Crown, but in 1794 when John Byng the diarist visited, it was The Hare & Hounds, and so it has remained.

While the beerhouse was more for the common labourer, the public house was, as its name implies, for all classes. There seems to have been a clear attempt to shape the leisure time and drinking habits of the villagers by the 3rd Lord Ongley. A report for a House of Lords Select committee in 1854 says of Old Warden,

I only found one drinking house there, and the people told me that drunkenness was nearly unknown. The steward of Lord Ongley (likely Matthew Reynolds) kept a drinking house, and he had provided various amusements for the people such as a gymnasium and cricket ground. Was there anything in the village to preclude anybody else starting a beershop or a public house? – I should say there was; it was Lord Ongley's own property. The fact was that drinking and drunkenness were unknown? Yes. You say that the public house was kept by Lord Ongley's steward, and subject to his Lordship's direction? Yes, subject to his supervision.

The researcher was clearly unaware of The Plough tucked away in Warden Street. The mention of a cricket ground offers no surprises, but the concept of a gymnasium is a revelation. Gyms were springing up all over the country in the mid-Victorian period, especially in public schools and civic parks in towns. Enlightened noblemen such as Ongley were providing healthy activity for their tenants as a counterbalance to the temptations of drink. In 1849 for example, the Earl of Ellesmere enclosed a park and provided a gym for the colliery workers and tenantry of his large estates. Gyms were often placed outside, and it seems that the gymnasium was probably the 'other instruments of pastime' noted by the visitor in 1848.

In 1901, a generous Frank Shuttleworth gave the men of the village their own recreation room, reflecting Ongley's earlier provision of gym and playground. There was probably more behind his generosity though; a need to provide some interest and relaxation to balance life in a small village against the 'bright lights' of the nearby towns that could entice men to move away and start new lives.

The Reading Room had two billiard tables, card tables for whist and cribbage and tables for dominoes and draughts. There was a separate committee room and a reading table for

The Reading Room, Old Warden

The reading and recreation room.

daily papers, weekly periodicals and monthly magazines. The room was open between 5 p.m. until 9 p.m. (no late nights encouraged here), and there were frequent 'smoking concerts' where live musical evenings were staged purely for the men. Whist and billiard competitions also took place. Of course, the new place of recreation was conveniently opposite the Hare & Hounds, and no doubt there was much movement between the two.

The first secretary was head gardener William Modral, and after Frank Shuttleworth's death in 1913, Richard, his young son, was elected president at the age of just three. The Reading Room is now the village hall, having been renovated and converted after much fundraising activity in the 1970s. The billiard tables were transferred to The Hut, which became the new snooker room.

The village has tried to field a good cricket team from as far back as 1839, when an Ickwell and Old Warden match was reported in the press. George and Frederick Ongley were among the supporters on Ickwell Green and Messrs Neal and Jackson (farmer and steward) were praised as 'truly excellent'. These sporting events provided a great day out for locals, and there is evidence that a band often added to the occasion. But fortunes varied; for example, in 1897, the vicar wrote sadly in the *Parish Magazine* that 'Our cricket adventures this year have not been to our credit'.

Ian Willis in his detailed history of Old Warden Cricket Club (2002), provides examples of entries in the surviving minute books which tell of the wider reach of the club within the village. He says,

> It becomes very clear when reading them (the minutes) that the cricket club was very much a focal point for the village, with whist drives and dances being held with such regularity that their popularity must have helped all the population ... to get through those hard winters of the 1930s and '40s.

The football club fared less well over the years. In 1897, the vicar reported that,

> The football club practically collapsed last season. Only eighteen members joined, twelve from Old Warden and six from neighbouring villages ... five have left the village, three are only resident during their vacations and one is past the age for play. The result has been that with great difficulty, a team has occasionally been provided for a home match, but scarcely ever for a match away from home. Is Old Warden content to disappear from the list of Football Clubs? Who will rise up to save us from such a disaster?

The club was not saved and at the end of 1897, a special meeting decided that too few young men were willing to support the team, so Old Warden could not compete with other clubs in the area. The club carried on providing practice and home games, and was later resurrected. In 1910, the village joined forces with Northill to become Northill and Old Warden United.

An interesting letter was sent to the *Bedfordshire Times* from South Africa in May 1935. It was from A. J. Endersby living at a house called 'Warden' in Cape Town. This was Arthur Endersby (born 1876), son of the village painter, plumber and glazier. He talks of fun and games in his youth:

Cricket Team, 1921.

I have seen marbles, tops, hoops, hare and hounds, paper-chasing, tipcat and leap frog in Bedfordshire ... in my boyhood days. When the late E. G. Capon (a Bedford man) was master of the Old Warden School we used to have paper chasing and soccer football on most moonlight nights. If the weather was unsuitable for outdoor games we played marbles in the village school after night school lessons were over. I might mention that the present very popular game of baseball was played on Old Warden cricket ground as far back as 1883/84. It was known to us as 'prisoners' base'.

The parish magazines provide some lovely descriptions of community entertainment. Magic Lantern exhibitions were extremely popular. Early in January 1901, Vaughan Lang, son of Revd Lang, displayed some slides of pictures taken by his brother, Col Eustace Lang, of the Boer War. The article says the slides 'gave a very interesting idea of the conditions of life during active service on the South African veldt ... included illustrations of many of the different types of guns used and also specimens of the native races.' There were also slides of Italy and Cambridge taken by the much travelled Eustace. A collection raised from this event went to the war fund.

Other entertainments included Revd Lang's 'Wheel of Life' or Zoetrope, which gave the impression of movement from still pictures. A conjurer, Mr Fred Culpitt, was a regular and used live rabbits in his show. Culpitt also gave a display of 'shadowgraphy', creating clever images with his hands. An impressionist also visited the village, a Mr Summer, whose portfolio included imitations of Henry Irving, black singers, a blue bottle and farmyard noises. Christmas festivities of 1898 produced a ventriloquist, Mr Osborne with his 'little friend Joey'.

In September 1926, Dorothy Shuttleworth produced a grand pageant, 'The Masque of Life', taking place over two days in the grounds of the park and Swiss Garden. The actors were her friends and family, servants, estate staff and many villagers. All proceeds were given to the Red Cross and Bedford Hospital. The masque was based on a charity event staged in London around 1907, with society figures, including Frank and Dorothy, taking the acting roles.

The Imperial Yeomanry camped in Old Warden Park in August 1902, just after it was formed. While the yeomanry gave displays of tent pegging and lawn cutting, a special programme of sports with money prizes was laid on for tenants and parishioners. Both children and adults enjoyed competing in the flat race, sack race, egg and spoon, wheelbarrow, hurdles and obstacle race. These very same events, including the hilarious three-legged race, were enjoyed by children at their school sports days right up to the 1960s. Indeed these innocent games were so popular that adults also carried on the theme at village fêtes, bringing in further fun activities such as a slow bicycle race and treasure hunts, using a peg to mark in a plot of ground, where the supposed treasure was buried.

After the Second World War, the village held regular whist drives and beetle drives, a game of dice with each number representing part of the beetle's body. Dances took place in the hut to the tunes of waltzes and quick steps.

Villagers were allowed to go fishing by permit on the two upper lakes of the park (the first of these now a reservoir). The Shuttleworth family also enjoyed skating on the lake during hard winters and punting in the summer months. The skating picture is from their visitor book, Frank Shuttleworth on the right.

At Queen Victoria's Coronation in 1838, newspapers reported various village celebrations, and in Old Warden emphasis was placed on feeding the poor; 'Warden – on Saturday last, Lord Ongley gave a quarter loaf, quart of beer and one pound and a half of beef to every poor person in this village, and half a quartern loaf, 1lb of beef and a pint of beer to every child.'

Sixty years later, the village celebrated Victoria's Diamond Jubilee with a fête organised by Frank Shuttleworth. All villagers and estate workers, over 200 people, were invited to 'an excellent dinner provided in a large tent at which Maj. Shuttleworth presided, assisted by Mrs Shuttleworth, Mrs Sibthorp (Caroline Shuttleworth's sister) and others'. During the dinner, the village children arrived 'in marching order, preceded by the band, and having sung a verse of the national anthem, continued their march through the gardens, and returned to a substantial tea in the tent'. Games followed for all closing, with a tug o' war for the men, and egg and spoon race for the women.

It was after this celebration that Caroline Shuttleworth presented a special book to all older children, and Jubilee mugs for the younger ones. The book, *The Queen's Resolve*, told the story of Victoria's life and was inscribed with the name of the village.

At the Coronation of Elizabeth II in 1953, a whole medley of events were planned for the day, including provision of a television, still a scarce luxury item.

The schoolroom held a village library, housed in fine oak library cupboards with wire mesh lockable doors, complete with catalogue and a regular changeover of books. Subscriptions in the late 1890s were 1d a month for schoolchildren, and 2d for others.

Beds County Council arranged various informative lectures for villages around the county. In Old Warden, a lecture on cottage gardening in 1897 covered fruit culture and insect pests. In 1898 came 'Homely Talks for Women' about the care and management of young children. Miss Allen's lectures included practical demonstrations such as dressing an infant, changing sheets and making poultices. The following year, Miss Allen gave a

Above: The Pageant, 1926.

Right: Skating on the lake (The Shuttleworth Trust).

PROGRAMME OF EVENTS

Tuesday, June 2nd

n.—DESPATCH OF A TELEGRAM of loyal congratulations to Her Majesty Queen Elizabeth II.

n.—CHURCH SERVICE preceded by ringing of the bells.

n.—TELEVISION in W.I. Hut.

m.—PARADE in Schoolyard for Fancy Dress, Children and Adults, march to Cricket Ground for judging and presentation of prizes.

m.—SPORTS on Cricket Ground for Children and Adults.

m.—TEA, which will be free of charge. Please bring own cups.

m.—TUG OF WAR.

m.—PLANTING OF COMMEMORATION TREES on Cricket Ground by Mrs. Shuttleworth.

6.45 p.m.—TAPPING THE BARREL OF BEER.

8.00 p.m.—DANCING in W.I. Hut.

9.00 p.m.—BROADCAST OF SPEECH made by Her Majesty.

10.00 p.m.—BONFIRE and FIREWORKS.

Saturday, June 6th

CRICKET MATCH.

4.00 p.m.—TEA FOR CHILDREN over 3 years of age and under 15 in W.I. Hut. It is regretted that it will be impossible to ask parents. Children in outlying districts (Froghall, Kings Hill, Hill Foot, The Tunnel and Warden Street) will be collected by car at 3.30 p.m.

5.00 p.m.—CINEMA SHOW.

6.30 p.m.—PRESENTATION OF CORONATION MUGS by Mrs. Shuttleworth.

The Coronation event programme, 1953.

Dorothy Shuttleworth presenting Coronation mugs at the school playing field. Estate agent Edward Bennett stands on left (Bedfordshire and Luton Archives).

course of 'first aid to the injured', and Vicar Lang hoped to arrange courses in dressmaking. In 1901 came 'hygiene and sick nursing'.

With the mobility afforded by the motorcar and railways, a trip to the seaside became a popular treat. All children who danced at Ickwell May Day were given a day trip to the seaside as a thank you, still remembered by a village child of the 1940s as such an exciting and unusual event for her. Dorothy Shuttleworth sent village families to her home at Sheringham in Norfolk for a week's holiday by the seaside, her chauffeur Charles Clarke driving the family there and back in style.

Walking in the village and the surrounding footpaths, field tracks and woods were enjoyed but rarely documented. Local walks included down the park (the footpath through the Whitbread estate), round the warren, up Queen Anne's, up the church, through Palmers Wood (particularly at bluebell time), round the Mount and to Sweetbriar, down the Slade and up Tobacco pipes; a simple pleasure for the taking in the beautiful countryside around Old Warden.

Sources

List of Abbreviations
BLA = Bedfordshire & Luton Archives
BHRS = Bedfordshire Historical Record Society
VCH = Victoria County History

Census Records 1841–1911 and British Newspapers 1710–1953 – 'Find My Past' website

Chapter 1
BLA ONG/180
www.eicships.info
www.historyofparliamentonline.org
Stanford, Caroline, *Queen Anne's Summerhouse History Album* (The Landmark Trust, 2009)
Richardson, Ellis, Tickell & Lawrence, *The Rolliad* (Google)
Northampton Mercury (September 1780 and July 1784)
The New Sporting Magazine (Vol. 1, May 1831)
'Old Warden and the Ongleys' (Beds County Council 1983 pamphlet)
BLA P105/28/1
The Journal of Horticulture and Cottage Gardener (1868)
The Sessional Papers printed by order of the House of Lords (1854)

Chapter 2
Diary of Colonel Weston Cracroft (unpublished) by kind permission of William Cracroft-Eley, the Hackthorn estate
www.gracesguide.co.uk
Buildings & Structures Research Report Swiss Garden, Victoria Hunns of Terre du Rocher (2012)
Whitakers Descendant Chart for Shuttleworth family of Gawthorpe
BLA CRT130/WAR
BLA Z186/53
Parish Magazines (1897, 1898 & 1901) (author's own)

Chapter 3
www.heritagegateway.org.uk/
National Archives Wills Index

BLA ONG/180
BLA X109/1
BHRS 81
BLA P105/8/1
Cain & Oliver, *The Tithe Maps of England and Wales* (1995)
BLA SL5/242

Chapter 4
BLA CRT120/15/15/10
BLA AT48 & MAT48

Chapter 5
BLA SD OldW14/1/5
BHRS 81
BLA CRT130/WAR16
BLA W1/849
BLA P69/2/1/1
BLA SL1/107
BLA SD OldW 1
BLA SD OldW 6/1-29
BLA CCX 25
Encyclopaedia Brittanica (Vol. 25, 1911)
Austin, Thomas George, *The Straw Plaiting and Straw Hat and Bonnet Trade* (1871)
BLA X698/1/1

Chapter 6
BLA P105/25/1
Cadell & Davies, *Bedfordshire* (1813)
BHRS 50
BLA P69/2/1/1
Huntingdon, Bedford & Peterborough Gazette (6 October 1827 and 27 September 1828)
BLA FAC107
BLA P105/25/4
BLA P69/2/1/5
Parish Magazines (1897, 1898 and 1901)
BLA P10/28/40
BLA SL7/6
Victoria County History Beds (Vol. 3, 1912)
BLA CRT130/WAR 10
BLA SD Old Warden1
BLA LF29/14
Beds Advertiser (12 January 1900)
BLA PC Old Warden1
BLA W/V 2/5

Beds Advertiser (24 August 1894)
BLA CRT150/211
BLA P105/2/1/4
BLA P105/2/2/4

Chapter 7
BLA SL5/253
Hickman, Neil 'The Forgotten One – LEL and the Poem in the Swiss Garden' – pamphlet
BLA P105/3/1

Chapter 8
BLA ONG/180
Northampton Mercury (14 December 1774 and 12 September 1829)
BLA P105/8/1
BHRS 50
BLA Gaol Records Database
Huntingdon, Bedford & Peterborough Gazette (1834)
Western Gazette (3 June 1910)

Chapter 9
BHRS 81
BHRS 79
BHRS 54
Z50/129/109
ABE2 (Vol. 1, page 179)
X65/61
BLA P105/28/1
BLA P105/3/1

Chapter 10
BLA W1/5508
Parish Magazines (1897, 1898 and 1901)
BHRS 71
BLA W/V 2/5
Storton, John Ernest, *Childhood Memories of Cople* (Cople village website)
BLA Z1310/3/1a-b
BLA SDOldW2/1
BLA SDOldW1/2
www.aircrewremembrancesociety.co.uk
BBC WW2 Peoples War Project Online
Biggleswade Chronicle Memory Lane

Chapter 11

C Bruyn Andrews (ed.), *The Torrington Diaries* (Vol. 4, Eyre & Spottiswood, 1938)

BLA 180/YOU

Gates, Barbara (ed.), *Journal of Emily Shore* (University Press of Virginia, 1991)

Nottinghamshire Guardian (1868)

BLA P105/28/1

Shuttleworth Family Visitor Books, (1884–1913)

BHRS 86

Yardley, Elizabeth, *A Motor Tour of France & England* (James Pott & Co., New York, 1911)

Chapter 12

BLA X65/61

Ickwell Mayday Internet

BLA CRT130/Northill21

BLA Old Warden Community Pages

BLA L12/154-155

Essex Standard & Eastern Counties Advertiser 6.8.1847

Parish Magazines 1897, 1898 & 1901

The Sessional Papers printed by order of the House of Lords (1854)

Bedfordshire Historical Record Society Publications

Agar, Nigel E., *The Bedfordshire Farm Worker in the Nineteenth Century*, BHRS 60 1981

Bell, P. (ed.), *Episcopal Visitations in Bedfordshire 1706–20*, BHRS 81 2002

Bushby, David, *The Bedfordshire Schoolchild*, BHRS 67 1988

Cirket, Alan F. (ed.), *Samuel Whitbread's Notebooks*, 1810–11, 1813–14, BHRS 50 1971

Pickford, Chris (ed.), *Bedfordshire Churches in the Nineteenth Century S-Y*, BHRS 79 2000

Smart, Richard (ed.), *The Bousfield Diaries*, BHRS 86 2007

Stockdale, Eric, *Law and Order in Georgian Bedfordshire*, BHRS 61 1982

Bibliography

Antrobus, Stuart, 'We wouldn't have missed it for the world', *The Women's Land Army in Bedfordshire 1939–50* (Book Castle Publishing)

Bayliss, Robert, *The Life Story of a Country Boy* (2010)

Bradford, Sarah, *George VI* (Penguin, 2011)

Darley, Gillian, *Villages of Vision* (Granada Publishing Ltd, 1978)

Dell, Simon, *The Victorian Policeman* (Shire Publications Ltd, 2008)

Desmond, Kevin, *Richard Shuttleworth; An Illustrated Biography* (Janes Publishing Co. Ltd, 1982)

Godber, Joyce, *History of Bedfordshire* (Bedfordshire County Council, 1984)

Hill, Sir Francis, *Victorian Lincoln* (Cambridge University Press, 1974)

Horn, Pamela, *The Victorian Country Child* (Alan Sutton Publishing Ltd, 1990)

Horn, Pamela, *The Real Lark Rise to Candleford* (Amberley Publishing, 2012)

Horn, Pamela, *Ladies of the Manor* (Alan Sutton Publishing, 1997)

Houfe, Simon, *Bedfordshire* (Pimlico, 1995)

Reay, Barry, *Rural Englands* (Palgrave Macmillan, 2004)

Ridley, Ursula (ed.), *Cecilia, The Life & Letters of Cecilia Riddle* (The Spredden Press, 1990)

Risby, Stephen, *Prisoners of War in Bedfordshire* (Amberley Publishing, 2011)

Shuttleworth, Dorothy, *Richard Ormonde Shuttleworth*

Strong, Roy, *A Little History of the English Country Church* (Vintage, 2008)

Whitbread, Sam, *Plain Mr Whitbread* (The Book Castle, 2008)

Wild, Trevor, *Village England* (I. B. Tauris & Co. Ltd, 2004)

Willis, Ian, *The History of Old Warden Cricket Club*